ART & DESIGN Workbook

for Junior Certificate

Gráinne McKeever

Specimen Copy
With the compliments of
Frances Kelly
Contact no: 086 2437751
Email: fkelly@gillmacmillan.ie   www.gillmacmillan.ie

Gill and Macmillan

Gill & Macmillan
Hume Avenue
Park West
Dublin 12
with associated companies throughout the world
www.gillmacmillan.ie

© Gráinne McKeever 2013

978 07171 5573 6

Design and print origination by Mike Connor Design & Illustration

The paper used in this book comes from the wood pulp of managed forests. For every tree felled, at least one tree is planted, thereby renewing natural resources.

All rights reserved.
No part of this publication may be copied, reproduced or transmitted in any form or by any means, without written permission of the publishers or else under the terms of any licence permitting limited copying issued by the Irish Copyright Licensing Agency.

Any links to external websites should not be construed as an endorsement by Gill & Macmillan of the content or view of the linked material.

For permission to reproduce photographs, the author and publisher gratefully acknowledge the following:

© Alamy: 20, 22, 38, 54, 62, 63, 64, 86; © Getty Images: 47.

The author and publisher have made every effort to trace all copyright holders, but if any has been inadvertently overlooked we would be pleased to make the necessary arrangement at the first opportunity.

Contents

Introduction 1

Drawing 2

Media 11

Ideas 12

The Elements of Art 13

The Principles of Design 15

Line 17

Shape 21

Colour 28

Tone 32

Form 36

Contour 38

Texture 40

Pattern 41

Balance 44

Space 47

Rhythm 54

Scale 55

Size	56
Emphasis	57
Unity	58
Composition	59
Proportion	63
The Junior Certificate Art Exam	70
Graphic Design	72
Logo	79
Packaging	81
Poster	83
Postage Stamps	86
Printmaking	88
Textiles	89
Book Cover	89
3D Studies	91
Art and the Community	92
Evaluation	93
Art Timeline	94

Junior Certificate Art & Design Workbook

Introduction

In this book you are going to learn all about the **elements of art** and the **principles of design** and how to use them in your work. This will help you to use your imagination to generate new ideas and encourage you to explore a variety of skills, techniques and media so that you can make better decisions when you are designing and creating works of art.

Throughout this course you are going to become more **visually aware**, that means you will take notice of the world you see, and start to notice how art and design affects your life and the world you live in.

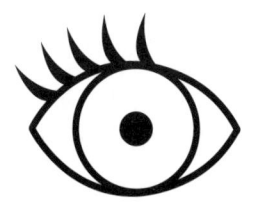

We all have our own ideas about what we think is stylish or appealing in terms of fashion, hair style, music etc. and we are free to create our own sense of style in our artwork too. This workbook will encourage you to develop your own style so that you can use the elements of art and the principle of design to express your own ideas. This book will give you the oppourtunity to record how these elements are present in our environment and everyday lives.

Activity Draw some images that represent your style in terms of fashion, music, film, your interests and hobbies.

Drawing

Drawing is the foundation of art and design. **Everybody can draw**, all you need is practice to become more confident and to develop your own unique style. It is important to remember that we are not seeking perfection in our drawings. Sketches are not finished pieces, they are tools to help us develop our skills so it is alright to make mistakes. **Do not erase** lines when you start drawing. It is hard to get any drawing done if you keep rubbing your work out and it will make you lose confidence in your ability. Instead, leave all lines until the end; you might be surprised at what you decide to keep.

When we draw we are recording **visual information**. In other words we are describing something using the elements of art and the principles of design. We are describing exactly what shape, size, colour etc. something is. In order to describe it accurately we need to observe it accurately, so take time to look closely at the object before you rush into drawing it. This is called **observational drawing**, and it gets easier when we train our hand to work at the same speed as the eye. We call this **hand-eye coordination**.

A fun way to practise hand–eye co-ordination is to use the technique of **blind drawing**. This is a method of drawing where you do not look at the page; instead, your gaze is always fixed on the object you are drawing. This helps your hand and eyes to work together at the same time. Your pencil is never lifted from the page and your eyes never leave the object you are drawing. This method of drawing is also called **continuous line drawing**. It helps you become more confident, as there is no pressure on you to create something 'perfect'. Sometimes we are tempted to add extra lines or details to sketches in order to make objects more recognisable. There is no need to do this in blind drawing: you simply draw the lines you actually see.

Activity Draw an object using the *blind drawing* or *continuous line drawing* method. Remember to look only at the object you are drawing: do not look at the page and do not lift the pencil at any time.

There are many other methods of drawing: analytical, gestural, imaginative, life and still life.

An **analytical drawing** is a detailed drawing made while looking closely and examining the object.

Activity Create an *analytical drawing*. Try using your pencil at different pressures to achieve hard and soft lines, as they appear on the object.

A **gestural drawing** is a simple drawing with very little detail. It includes only the essential lines that are necessary to capture the object. Gestural drawings indicate the volume of the object, its size and shape; they are often quick and sketchy.

Activity Create a *gestural drawing*.

An **imaginative drawing** is a drawing created from memory or imagination. Sometimes imaginative drawings combine reality with memory or imagination; sometimes not.

Activity Create an *imaginative drawing*.

Junior Certificate Art & Design Workbook

A **life drawing** is a drawing created from observation of a person.

Activity Create a *life drawing*. Ask a classmate, family member or friend to be your live model. Draw either head and shoulders, or a full figure.

A **still life drawing** is a drawing of real objects often specially set up in a display in order to be observed and drawn.

Activity Create a *still life drawing*. You can draw a display in full or you can choose a smaller section to draw. Use a viewfinder (see p.60) or your hands to choose the area you wish to draw.

Junior Certificate Art & Design Workbook

When drawing, you will encounter man-made objects and organic objects. **Man-made objects** tend to have lots of straight lines, angles and geometric shapes. **Organic objects** tend to have less structure and a more organic shape.

Activity Make a list of the man-made and organic objects you could draw.

Man-made

_____

_____

_____

_____

_____

Organic

_____

_____

_____

_____

_____

Activity Identify which of the following objects are organic and which are man-made.

9

Mark-making

As children, the first experience we have of drawing is **mark-making**. It is as important now as it was then to experiment with creating a variety of marks. In time, this will help you to communicate different ideas in a visual way.

Activity — Try using the following tools for mark-making in your sketch pad or journal:

- string and ink
- paint and a twig
- a paintbrush and juice
- charcoal

Drawing can be done on any surface with any variety of **materials**, including:

- vellum (animal skin) and crushed leaves or berries
- canvas and paint
- the ground and chalk
- tree bark and a knife
- cave wall and a rock
- wallpaper and crayons

Drawing has become more accurate and realistic with the development of proportion, perspective and composition (which will be examined later in this book). Over time, it has also gained freedom of expression. There is no limit to the potential of your drawing, but it does take patience and practice.

Activity — Think of other materials you could use.

_____

_____

_____

Media

In Junior Certificate Art, you will learn how to use many different **media** – some traditional and some experimental.

Pencils are graded on a continuum from H (for hardness) to B (for blackness). H pencils are harder, so they make a lighter mark; B pencils are softer, so they make a blacker mark (e.g. 6B is blacker than 2B).

Activity — Shade the boxes below, using different grades of pencils for different effects.

Activity — Use your pencils to blend areas, smudge and create cross-hatch patterns.

Paper is made by pressing together moist fibres (typically pulp) derived from wood, rags or grasses. It is characterised by weight. Cartridge paper is high-quality paper used for drawing. Paper comes in standard sizes. A typical refill pad is A4; double this size is A3; double that size is A2; etc. Similarly, half the size of A4 is A5; half this size is A6; etc.

Other media you might use include: **chalk pastels**, **charcoal**, **oil pastels**, **markers** and **inks**. **Paint** can be poster paint, acrylic paint or oil paint. These are made with water, plastic or oil, respectively.

It is possible to experiment with many different media. You can: use found objects to create collages; draw with sticks dipped in ink; mix sand into your paint; or even paint with crushed berries or mud!

Ideas

In order to fuel your imagination, it is important to keep a record of your thoughts and ideas. You can then develop them for your art and design work. This is where your journal or sketch pad comes in! This will be the place where you explore your ideas visually and investigate and experiment with new techniques and media, as well as practising your skills.

A good starting point is a **mind map**. To create a mind map, draw a spider diagram and write your theme in the centre. Then let your imagination run with all of the words and images that come to mind in relation to that theme. This will help to develop creativity and originality in your work.

Activity Imagine that you are planning a project on one of the following themes: **transport, holidays, food, hobbies, music, entertainment, sport, family, community, people, workplaces, books, poetry, environment or animals.**

Choose one theme and create a mind map for it.

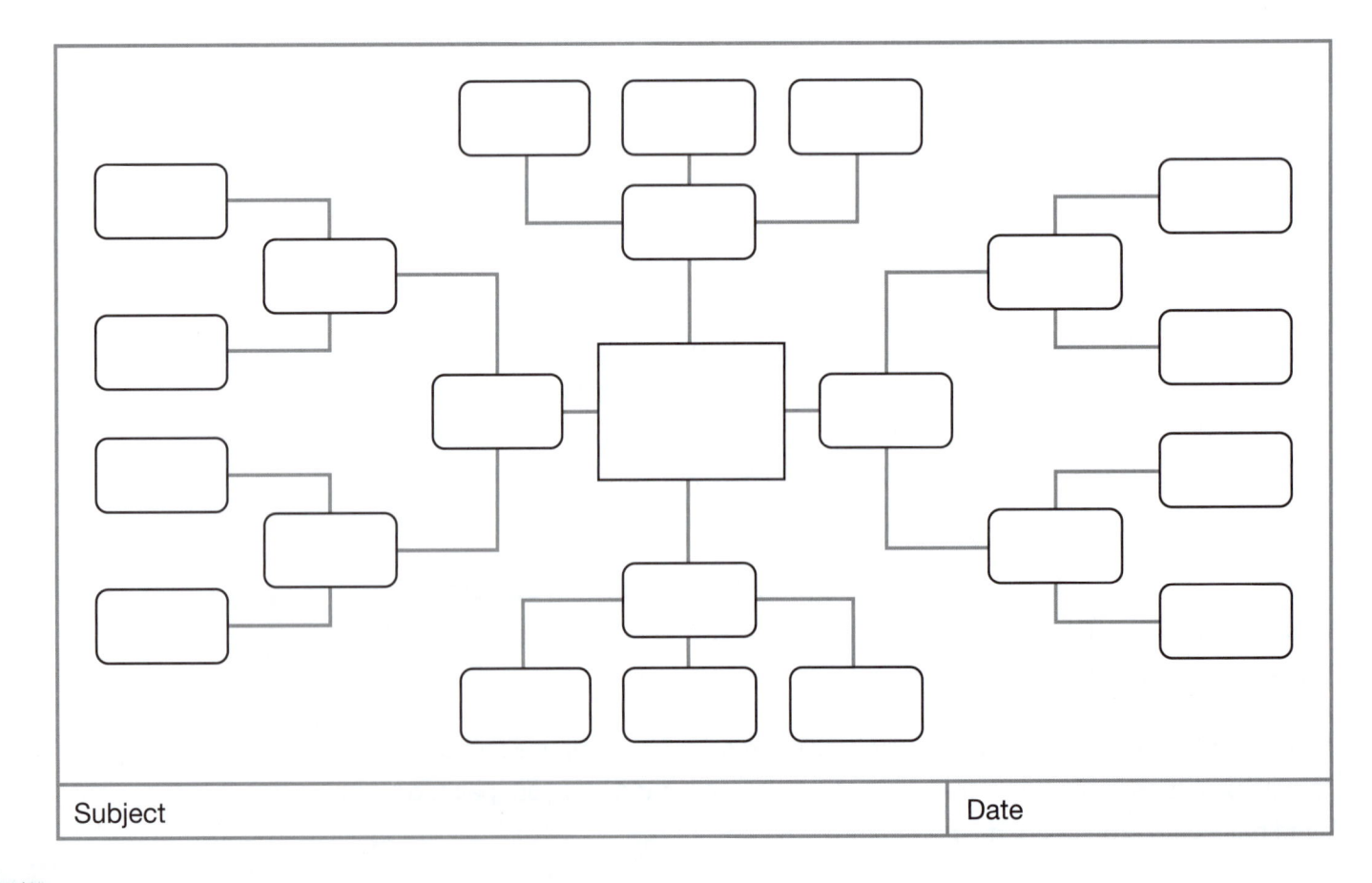

Subject	Date

The Elements of Art

The visual arts involve art forms such as painting, drawing, printmaking, sculpture, ceramics, design, crafts, photography and film. Within each art form are individual artworks; and each artwork is made up of certain elements.

You will be familiar with the **elements of art** and how to create them. This book will help you to develop your understanding of them and how best to use them to express your ideas. This will reinforce your art experience and extend your creative and critical abilities.

The elements of an artwork include:

- line
- shape
- colour
- tone
- form
- contour
- texture
- pattern

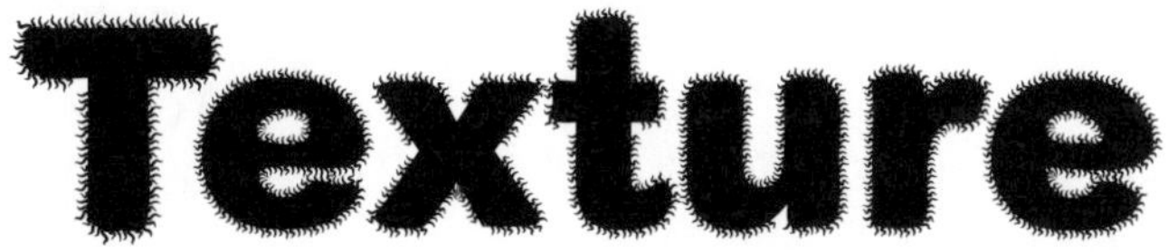

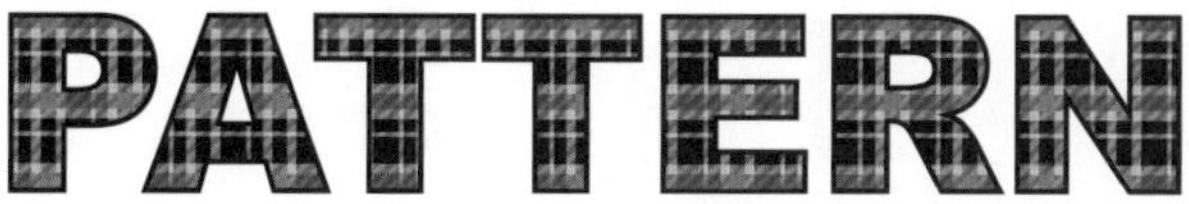

Activity The *elements of art* are explored in more detail on pp.17–43. When you have read the section on each element, return to this page and fill in a definition for the element below.

LINE

SHAPE

COLOUR

TONE

FORM

CONTOUR

TEXTURE

PATTERN

The Principles of Design

Design means planning, organisation and arrangement of parts. An effective design is one in which the **elements of art** and the **principles of design** have been combined to achieve an overall sense of unity.

Areas of design include: fashion and textiles, graphic design, web design, industrial design, product design, interior design and architecture. Take a look at your surroundings right now and you'll notice so many things that have been designed by either a product designer, interior designer, fashion designer or architect.

The principles of design include:

- balance
- space
- rhythm
- scale
- size
- emphasis
- unity
- composition

Junior Certificate Art & Design Workbook

Activity The *principles of design* are explored in more detail on pp.44–62. When you have read the section on each principle, return to this page and fill in a definition for the principle below.

BALANCE _____

_____

SPACE _____

_____

RHYTHM _____

_____

SCALE _____

_____

SIZE _____

_____

EMPHASIS _____

_____

UNITY _____

_____

COMPOSITION _____

_____

Line

Line is one of the elements of art. It is the path of a moving point. Line can be a means of communication, an element with which we can express our thoughts and feelings.

- **Horizontal line** can indicate calm and rest.
- **Vertical line** can show strength, perhaps growth.
- **Curves** can create a feeling of smoothness.
- **Diagonals** can give a sense of movement.
- **Zigzags** can indicate a feeling of agitation.

Line can create texture, shape, form, contour, pattern, rhythm and space.

- **Gestural lines** are quickly-drawn lines that describe the essential elements of an object. They give an indication of the object's weight, volume, action and movement. They convey character.
- **Continuous line** is an uninterrupted line that may cross over itself many times within one drawing.
- **Directional line** can lead the viewer's eye in a path through a composition.

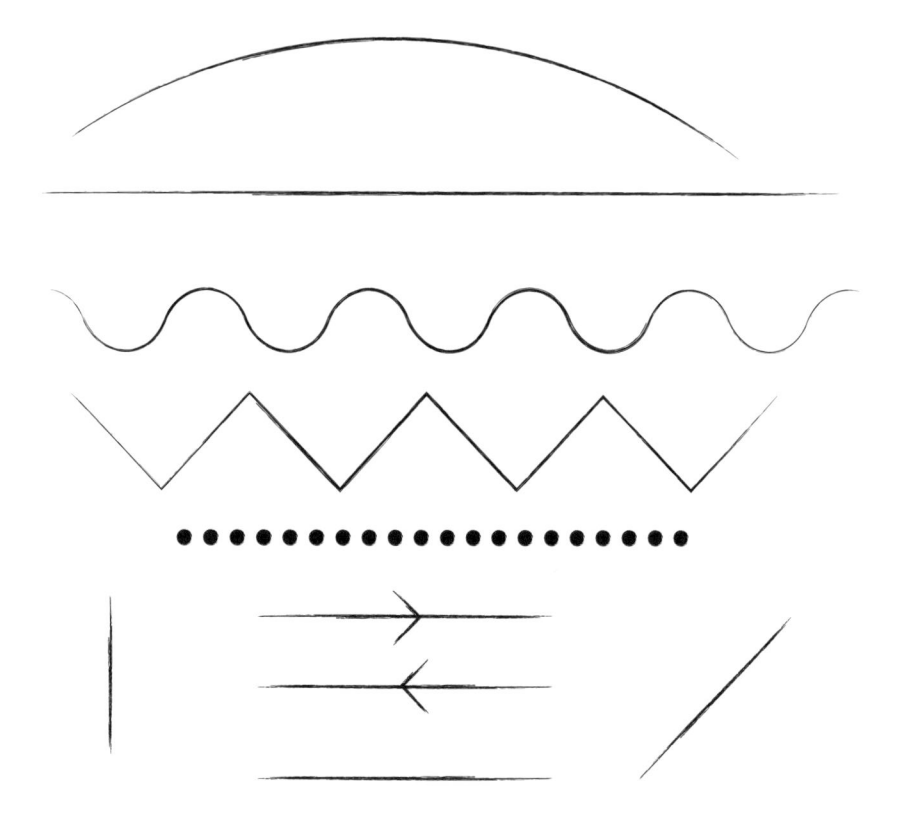

Activity Natural objects have interesting lines, e.g. an onion, a mushroom, a cabbage, an orange segment, leaves or waves. Draw some natural objects below.

Activity Examine the list of words in the box below. Try to convey the meaning of each word through *line*. Use pencils at different pressures and speeds. Try different media, such as markers or colouring pencils. It doesn't matter if some of your lines overlap or even move off the page!

FAST	ALTOGETHER
SLOW	STRAIGHT
HARD	LOOPY
SOFT	LOUD
ROUGH	QUIET
SMOOTH	CALM
LONG	ANGRY
SHORT	CLEAN
BIG	MESSY
SMALL	PARALLEL
THICK	WEIRD
THIN	NORMAL
BROKEN-UP	

There are many different ways we can use line to convey our ideas about the way we see something. Line helps us to express ideas in our drawing. When we begin drawing, it can be difficult to represent objects accurately. However, with practice, our hand will learn to move in sync with our eye and we will be able to record what we see.

Examples of artworks that use line include the stone carvings at Newgrange, the prehistoric monument in Co. Meath. The spirals, triskeles, chevrons and lozenges are abstract designs.

Activity Draw a variety of abstract lines.

Shape

A shape is a space which has been enclosed by other elements such as line or tone.

- **Squares and rectangles** can be associated with stability.
- **Circles and curved shapes** suggest movement and continuity.
- **Triangles** can lead the eye in an upward movement.
- **Inverted triangles** tend to give a sensation of imbalance and tension.

Shape is particularly important in composition (the placement or arrangement of elements in a work of art). There are geometric and organic shapes.

Geometric shapes are mathematical, with straight lines and angles.

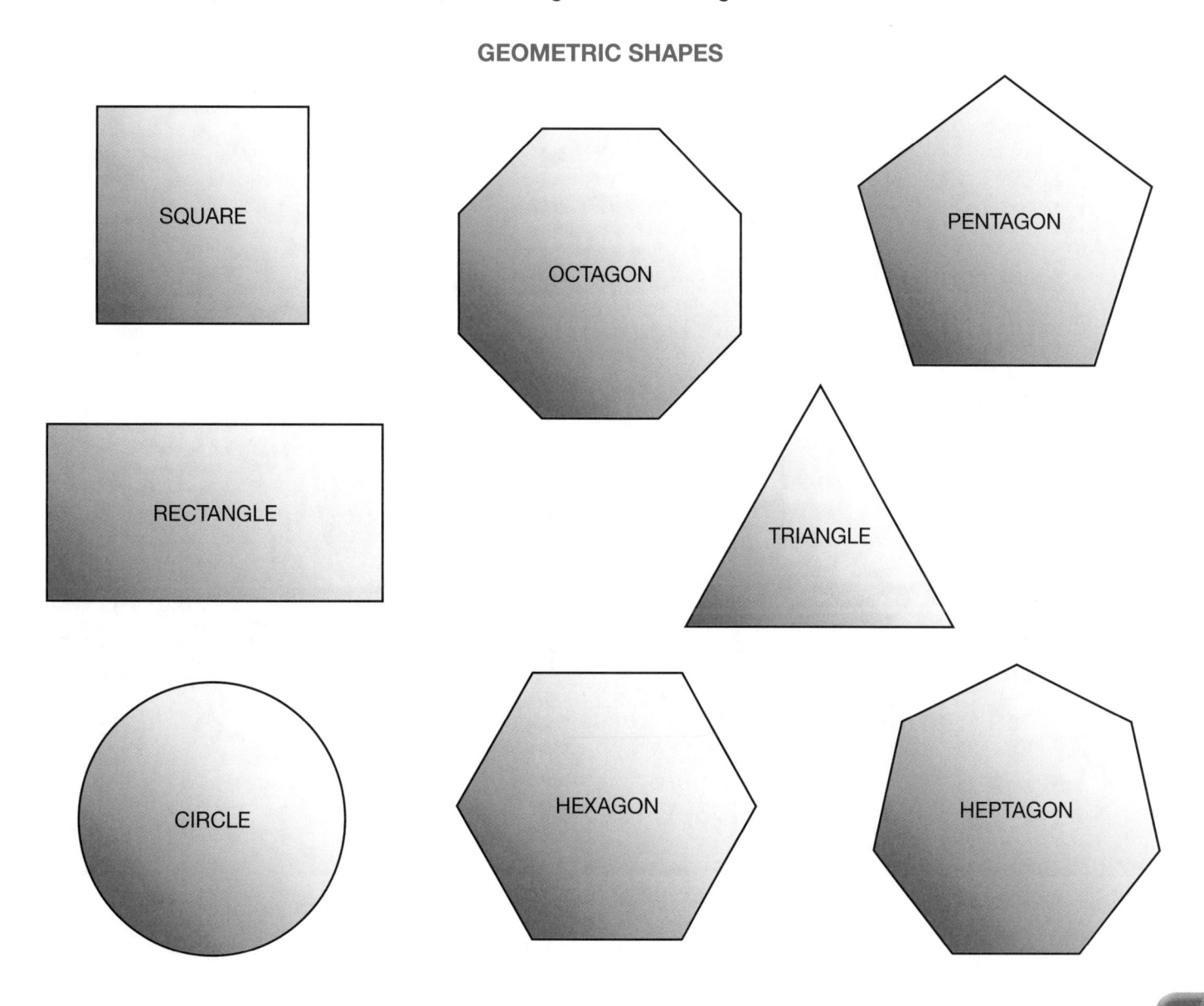

GEOMETRIC SHAPES

SQUARE

OCTAGON

PENTAGON

RECTANGLE

TRIANGLE

CIRCLE

HEXAGON

HEPTAGON

Organic shape does not have the same structure. It doesn't necessarily have straight lines or angles.

Aboriginal people are the indigenous people of Australia and they have used organic shape in their artwork for thousands of years. They painted on rock faces and cave walls and decorated their musical instruments and weapons. Today, Aboriginal artists are recognised for their unique style; and they exhibit their work in galleries around the world. A frequent subject of their work is the **Dreamtime**: the time when, they believe, spirits of animals created the earth.

Below is an example of an Aboriginal artwork. The dotting is a feature unique to Aboriginal art. In the past, Aboriginal people used natural materials from the bush to colour their artworks, e.g. berries, crushed rocks and plants. The use of these natural, earthy colours continues today. Aboriginal artworks are full of yellow, orange, red and brown, as well as some purple, black and white.

Activity Examine this Aboriginal drawing, which has a mixture of organic and geometric shapes. Can you identify the geometric shapes? Try to develop and colour the artwork.

When we draw from observation, shape can be a very useful tool. If we are able to identify various shapes in our environment, it makes it easier for us to break down complicated objects into several smaller shapes. Look at the Georgian doorway below, for example. It seems like quite a complicated drawing, but really it is just a series of simple geometric shapes put together.

Activity Draw a copy of the Georgian doorway in the box below. Finish the drawing by adding organic shapes, in the form of trees, pets, birds or flowers.

Positive and Negative Shape

Positive shape is the shape of an actual image and **negative shape** is the shape of the space left over. Look at the optical illusion below. The positive space shows a vase, while the negative space shows two people facing each other. Both spaces are equally important!

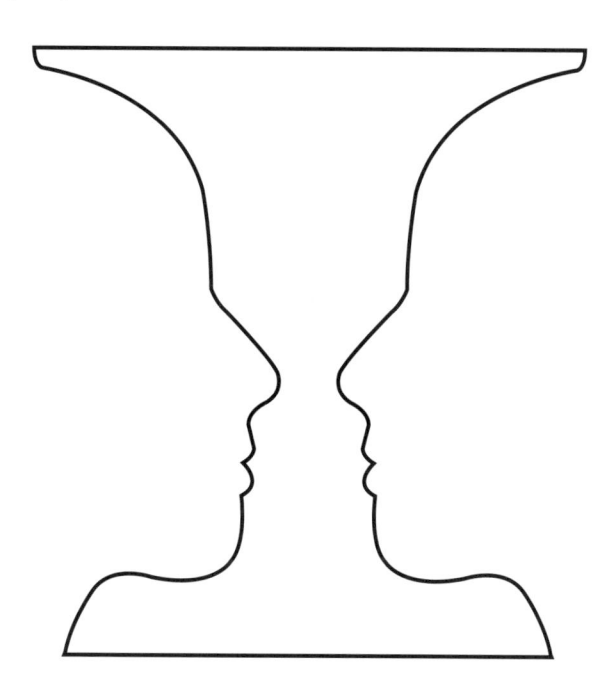

Activity — What can you see in this optical illusion? Add colour to it.

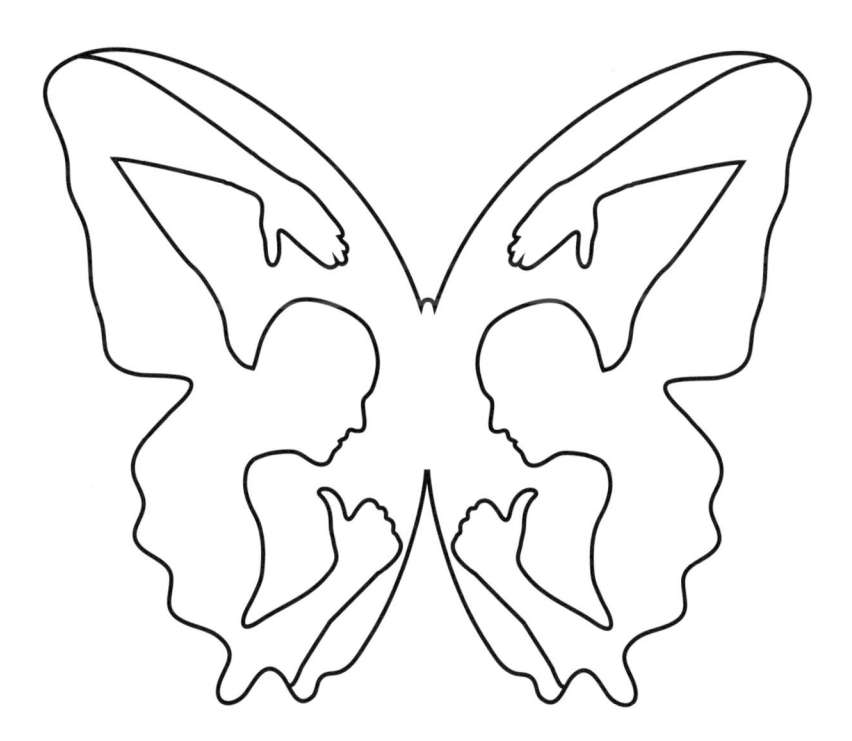

25

The **silhouette** is an art form that dates from the eighteenth century. It was popular for creating images of royalty before the invention of photography.

Activity Create silhouettes! Draw a face in profile on a piece of card. Cut the card very carefully along the profile and keep both pieces of the cut card. You will have two silhouettes: one in positive space, the other in negative space. Glue the silhouettes in the boxes below.

Junior Certificate Art & Design Workbook

Colour

A **prism** is an object that refracts light; it can break up white light into its spectrum of colours. A rainbow is a good example of this: the raindrops act as prisms, dividing light into the seven colours we recognise as a rainbow.

Glass objects with three or more sides act as prisms.

Activity Fill in the colours of the prism below.

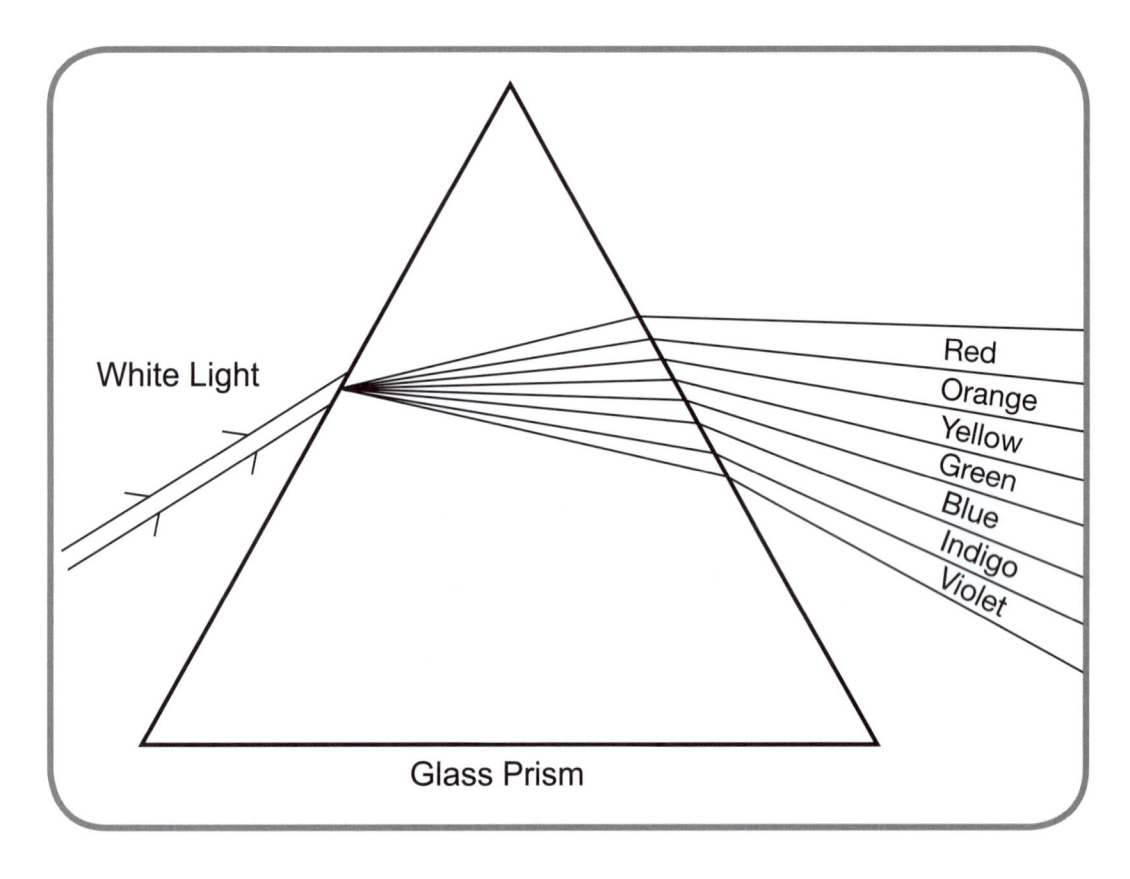

White Light

Red
Orange
Yellow
Green
Blue
Indigo
Violet

Glass Prism

The colours of the rainbow can be remembered with this mnemonic: **R**ichard of **Y**ork **g**ave **b**attle **i**n **v**ain (red, orange, yellow, green, blue, indigo and violet).

In 1666, Sir Isaac Newton proved beyond doubt that white light is a mixture of colours. He invented a disc of colour, which later became known as the Newton disc. It is a pie chart with seven segments showing the colours of the rainbow. When it is spun at high speed, the colours merge into white.

Activity Make your own Newton disc using white card and markers.

The Colour Wheel

The colour wheel is a pie chart of the primary, secondary and tertiary colours.

Primary colours are colours with which we can create almost any other colour.

Activity Fill in the primary colours.

RED	BLUE	YELLOW

Secondary colours are colours created when two primary colours are mixed together.

Activity Fill in the secondary colours. Think about which primary colours are used to create each secondary colour.

PURPLE	GREEN	ORANGE

Tertiary colours are colours created when one primary colour is mixed with either one or two secondary colours. For example, yellow mixed with green creates yellow-green. (It is called yellow-green because the colour it is mostly made of is yellow.)

Activity Use colouring pencils to fill in the colours below. Blend yellow and green to create yellow-green.

YELLOW	YELLOW-GREEN	GREEN

Complementary colours are colours opposite each other on the colour wheel. Because there is no component of one in the other, they pair really well and tend to stand out when placed next to each other. Complementary colours are often used in advertising and product packaging.

Activity Colour in the wheel below. Use colouring pencils so that you can blend and create the tertiary colours.

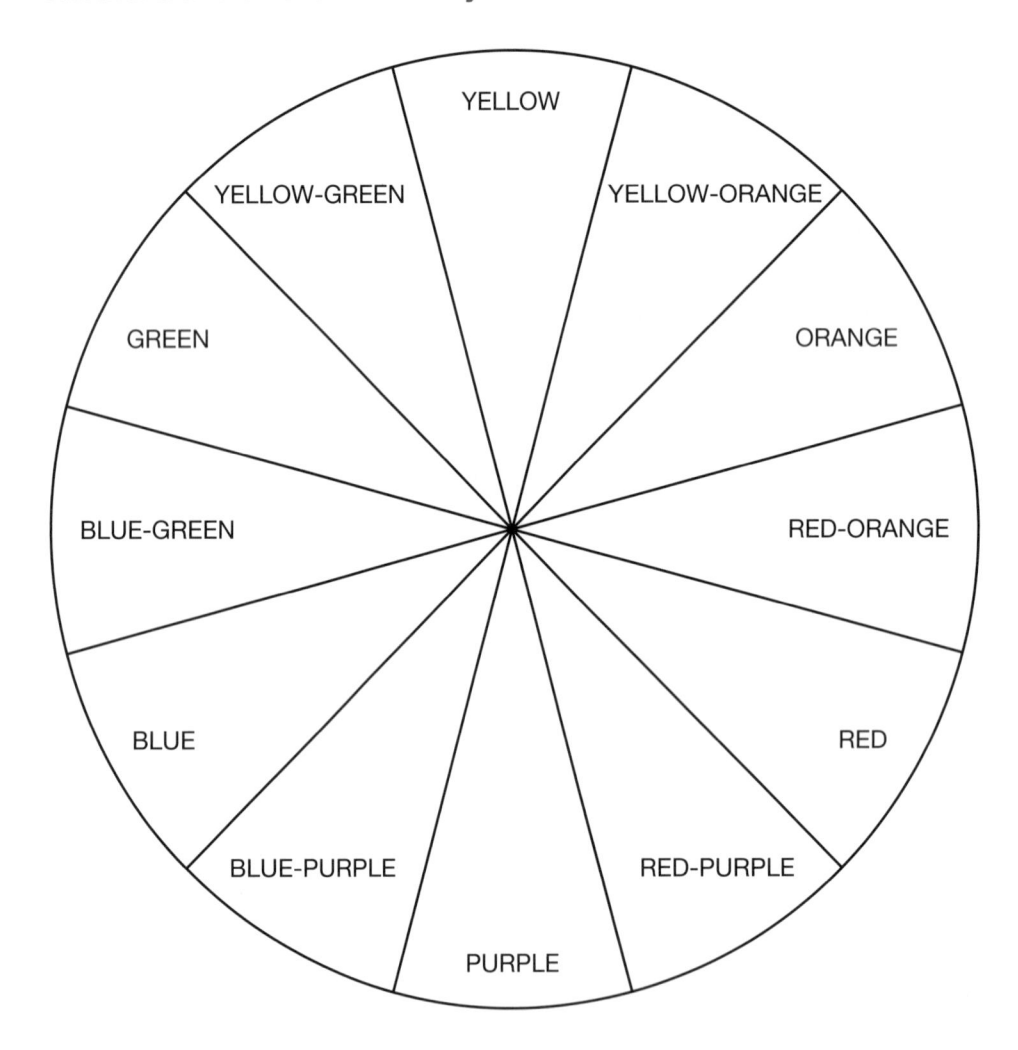

Activity Find the complementary colour for each of the following:

RED   _____

BLUE   _____

YELLOW   _____

Colour Values

The **values** of a colour refer to its **tint** and **shade**. A **tint** occurs when a colour is mixed with **white**. A **shade** occurs when a colour is mixed with **black**.

We describe colours as **warm**, **cool** or **neutral**. Red is a warm colour. Blue is a cool colour. Yellow is a neutral colour.

Colour Schemes

A colour scheme refers to the choice of colours used in design. A **monochromatic** colour scheme uses different values (tints and shades) of one single colour. See the tone chart on the next page for an example. An **analogous** colour scheme uses several different colours that appear next to each other on the colour wheel.

Activity Use colouring pencils to show a monochromatic colour scheme.

Activity Use colouring pencils to show an analogous colour scheme.

Tone

Tone is often referred to as 'shading' in artworks and means the variation of light and dark. It involves darkening areas that are in shadow and leaving other areas light. It is often used to produce illusions of dimension and form.

Tone may be used to:

- create pictorial structure by balancing areas of light and dark
- convey harmony or disunity
- indicate dramatic contrast
- give the illusion of solidity
- suggest qualities of light
- evoke a sense of space and distance
- compose rhythms across a picture or construction

Activity This tone chart displays the variety of values from black to white. Shade in the empty column and try to match the tones on the left.

Junior Certificate Art & Design Workbook

Activity Carefully examine your own hand. Which areas are lightest in tone and which are darkest? What tones appear in between? Add tone to the image below.

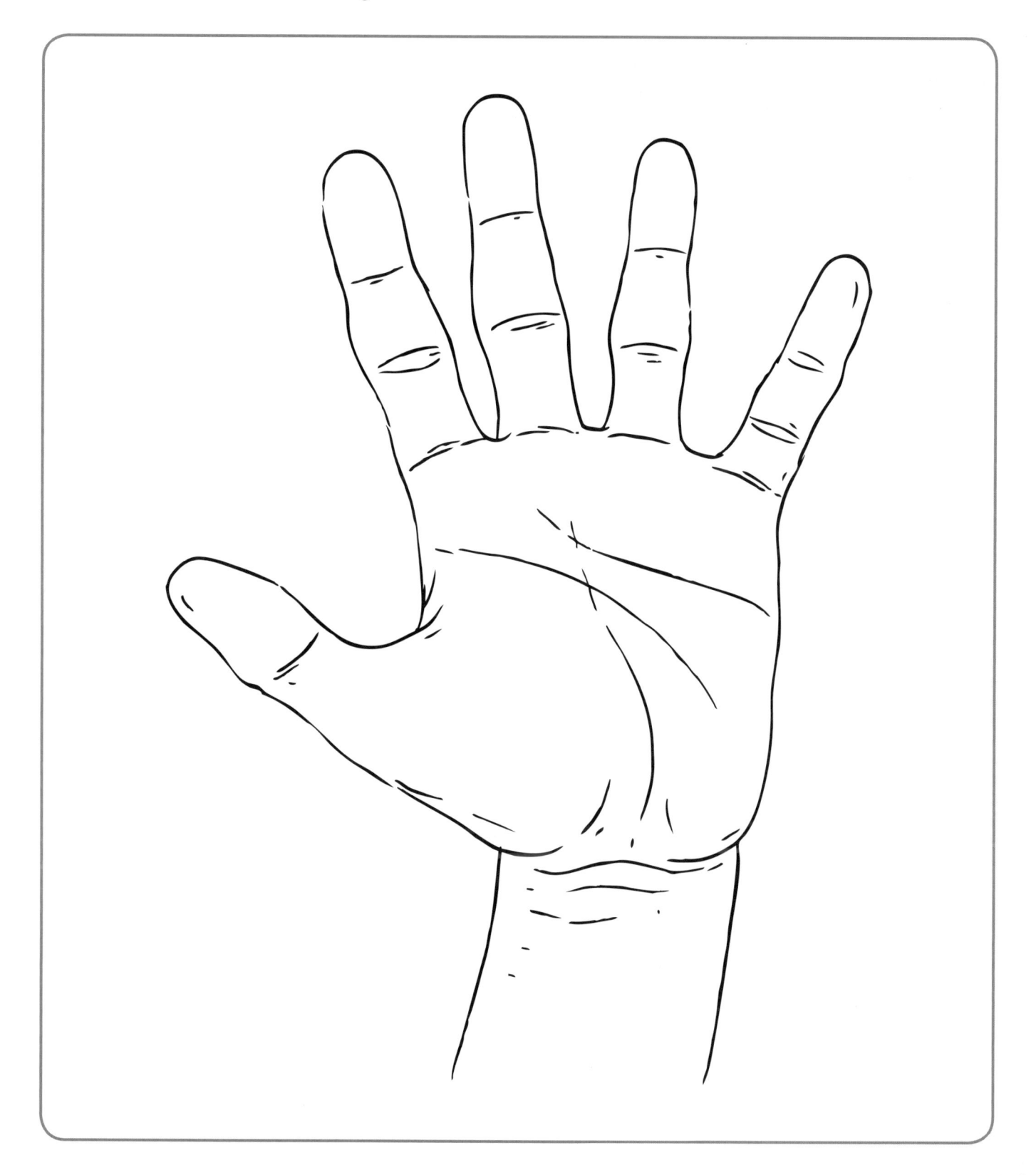

33

Junior Certificate Art & Design Workbook

The human face is very interesting in terms of tone. Our skin is generally the same colour all over. However, because different facial features protrude and recess, we look as though there are many different tones of the same colour on our face.

Activity

Examine your face in a mirror. Which areas of your face catch the light and which are in shadow?

What happens if you change the direction of the light source, e.g. the position of your face in relation to a window or light bulb?

What happens if you move closer to the light source, or further away?

Use colouring pencils to add tone to the face below.

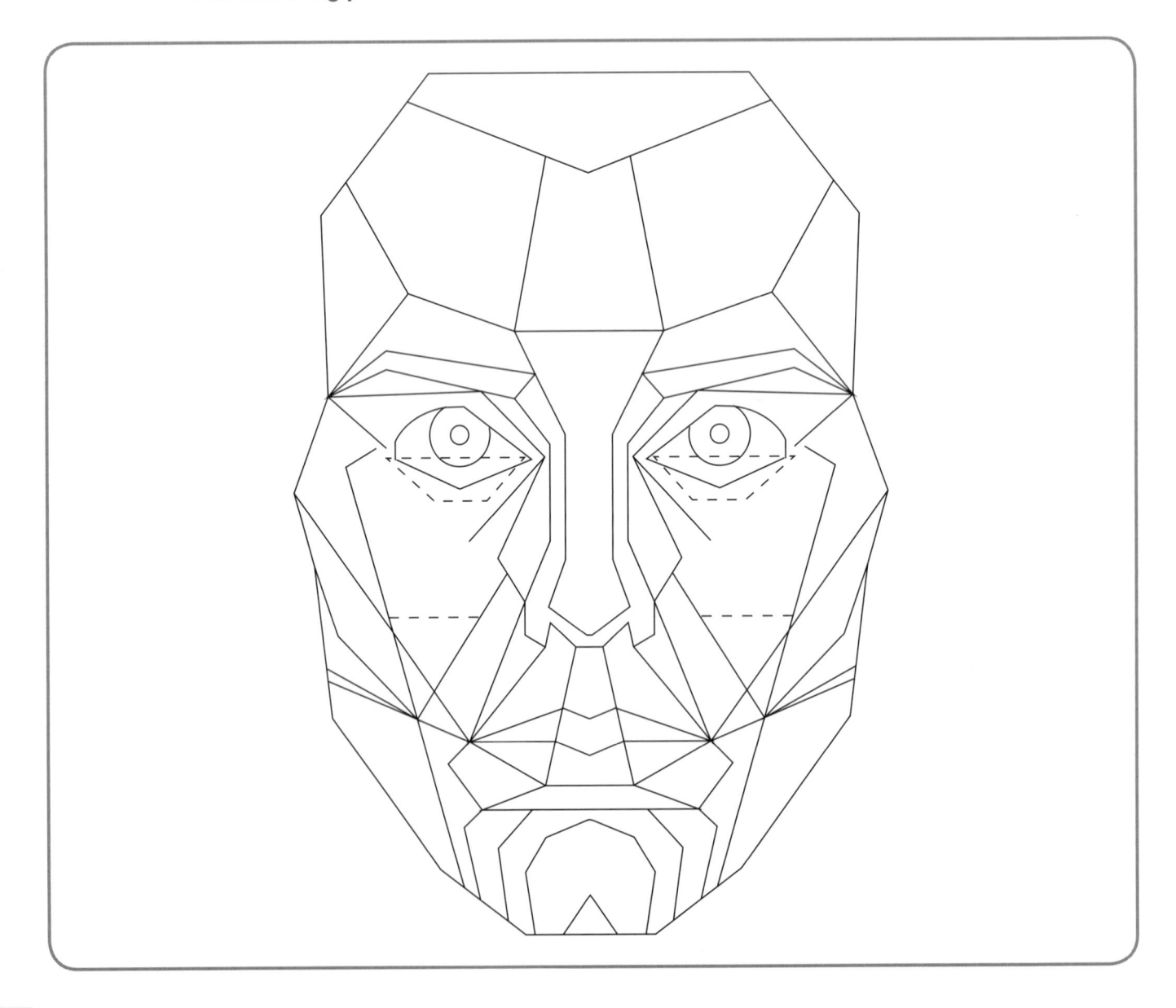

34

Caravaggio was an Italian artist of the Renaissance era and he used tone to great effect. One of his most famous paintings is *The Taking of Christ* (c.1602); it hangs in the National Gallery of Ireland, Dublin.

Caravaggio used a very special style of tone called **chiaroscuro**. It is an Italian term, which literally means 'light-dark'. *Chiaroscuro* is characterised by a strong contrast between light and dark.

Activity Find an image of Caravaggio's *The Taking of Christ* and glue it in the box below.

The Taking of Christ depicts the moment that Christ is taken by the Roman soldiers after being betrayed by Judas. Caravaggio painted himself in the artwork: he is the onlooker holding a lamp. The painting has an interesting history. The original was thought to be lost but was discovered hanging in the dining room of the Jesuit Community on Lesson Street in Dublin in the early 1990s. It was only when the Jesuit Community decided to have the painting restored that they discovered it was the original Italian masterpiece. The painting is on permanent loan from the Jesuit Community to the National Gallery of Ireland, Dublin.

Form

Form is the element of art that is concerned with **dimension**. When we draw on a page, it is a two-dimensional representation of an object that, in reality, has **form** or **three dimensions: length, width** and **depth** (e.g. a swimming pool).

Shape is two-dimensional or **2D**; **form** is three-dimensional or **3D**. By adding **tone** to a shape we can create the illusion of a 3D object on a 2D surface.

Activity Add tone to these shapes to create the illusion of form.

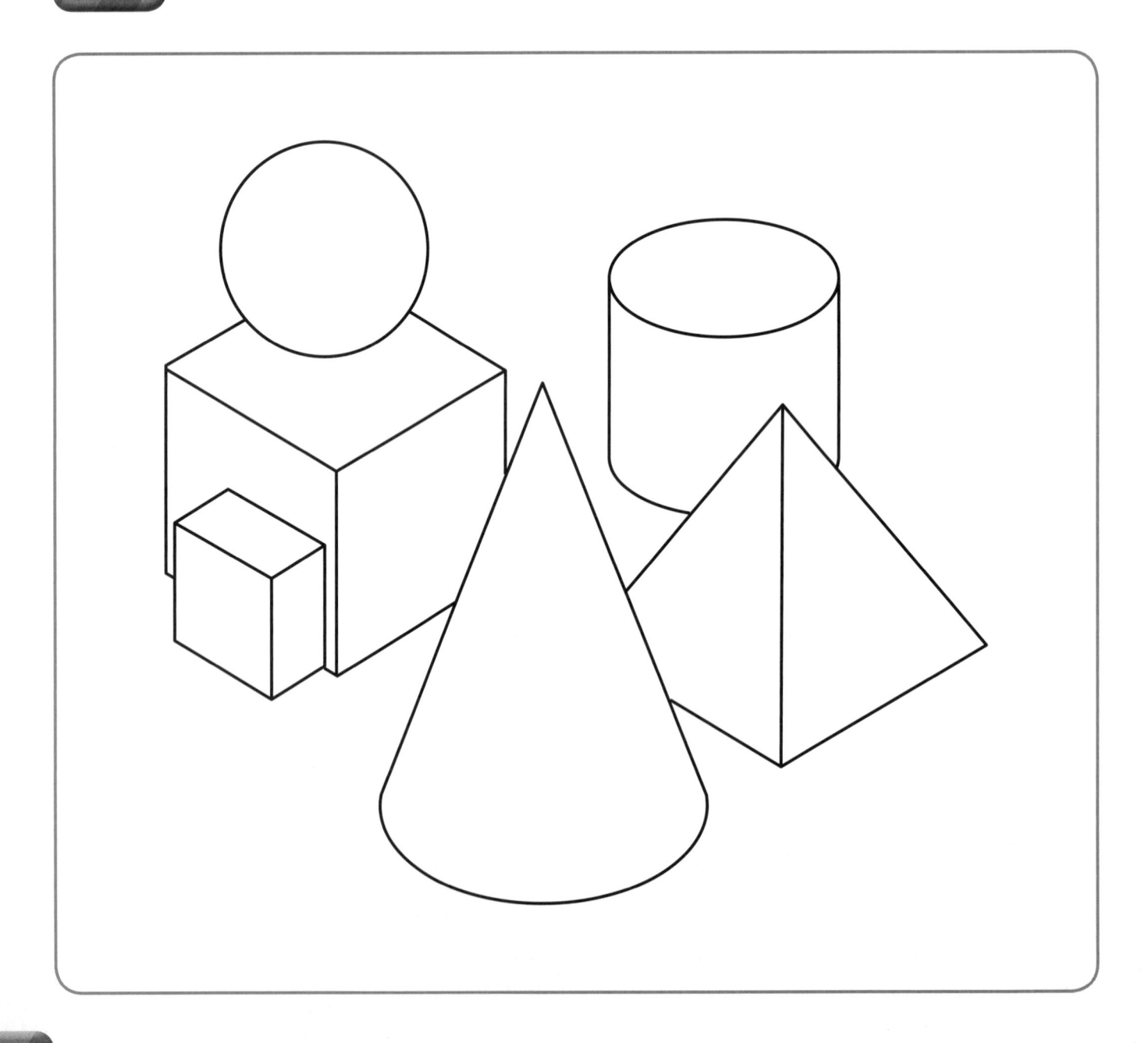

Activity Create forms based on these templates. You can make them with card and masking tape.

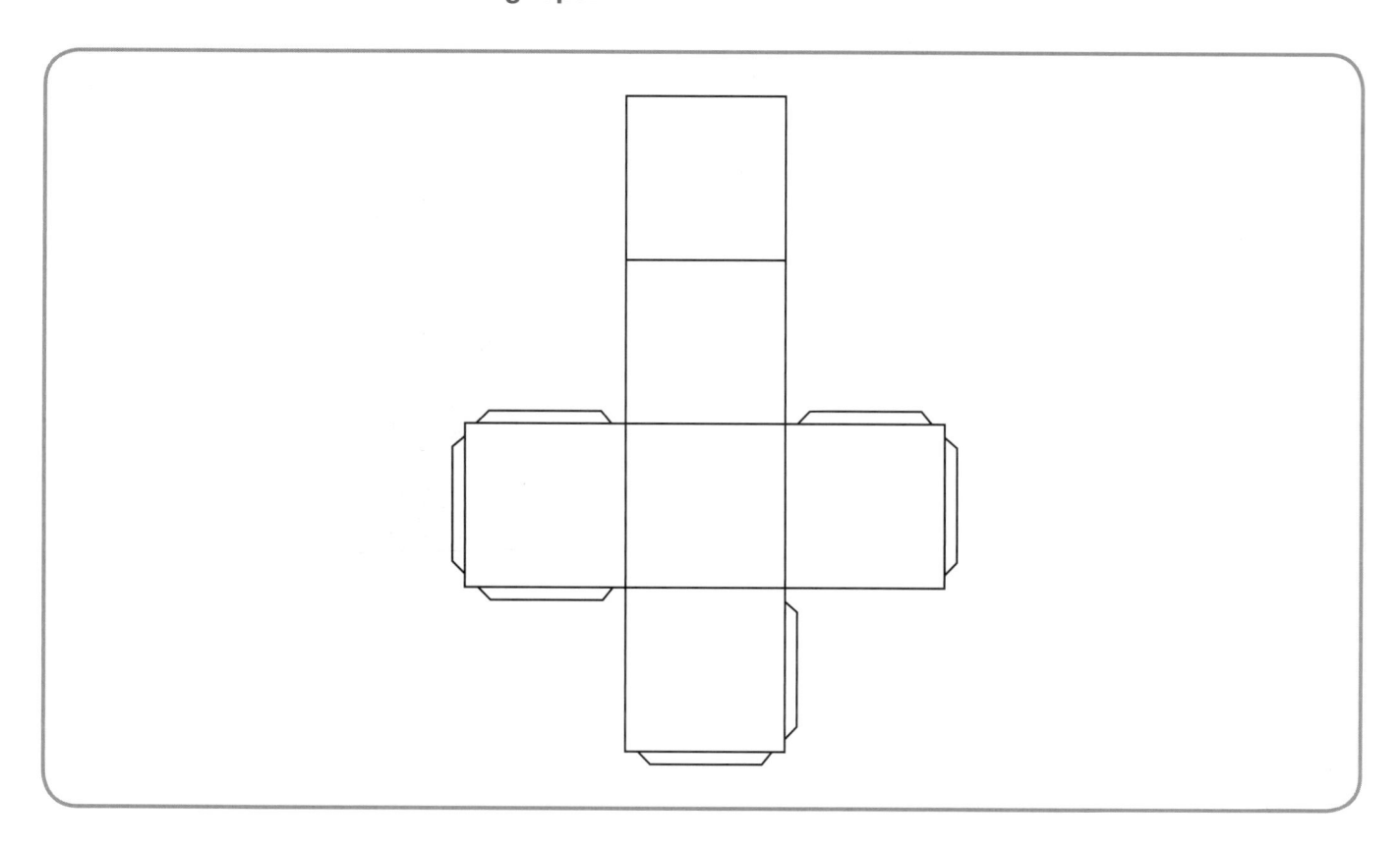

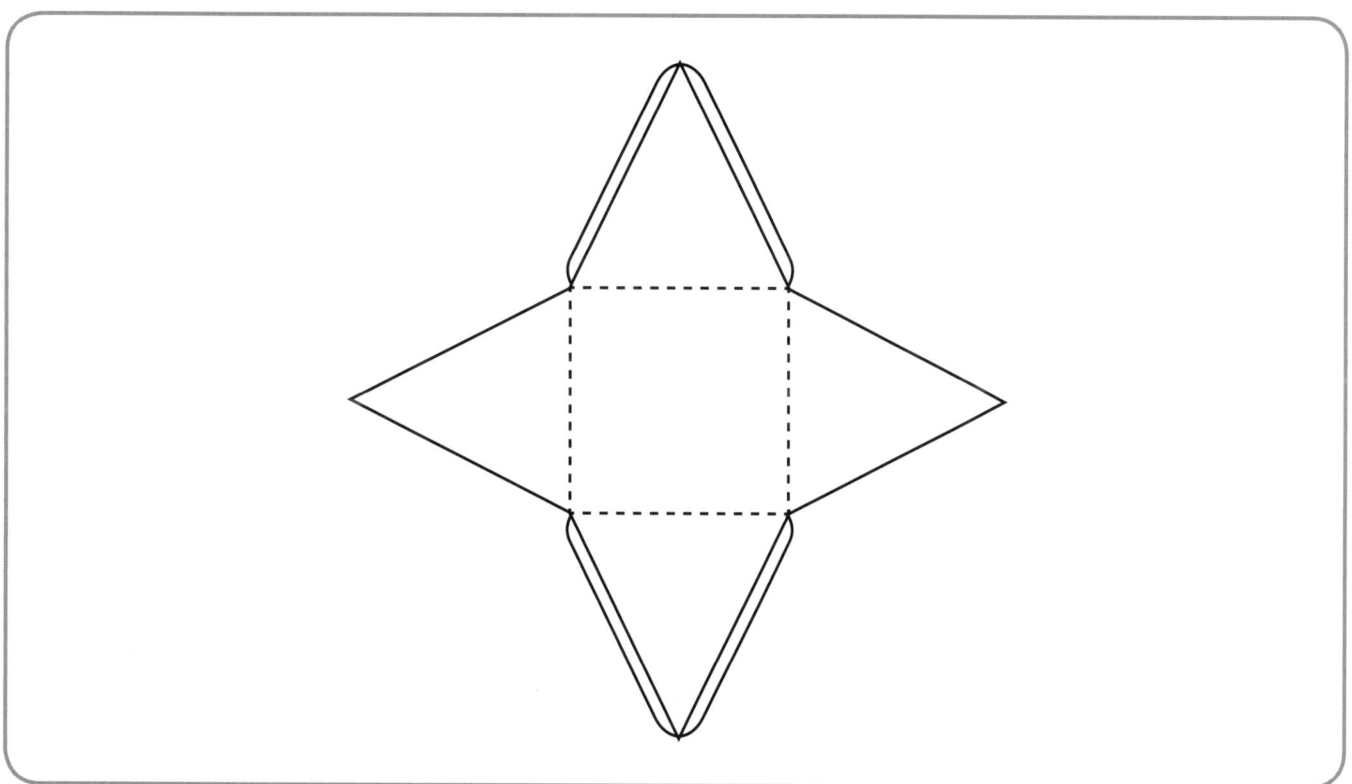

Contour

Contour is an element of art that refers to the *use of line*. **Contour lines** are lines that define the edges of a subject, giving it **volume** and indicating form. Contour is not to be confused with outline, which is the shape of the object.

A cola bottle is a good example of how contour lines give a clear indication of the form of the bottle.

Activity Draw the contours of a sphere, cylinder or cone.

Activity Draw an object, using contour lines to show its form and volume, e.g. a shoe, a bottle or a piece of fruit.

Texture

Texture refers to the surface quality of an object or material, i.e. how it feels to the touch. We can respond to texture visually (non-tactile texture) or we can respond to texture by touch (tactile texture).

The following words describe different textures:

- rough
- smooth
- woolly
- fluffy
- furry
- bristly
- silky
- slimey
- greasy
- grainy
- soft
- hard

Activity Give examples of objects that represent these textures.

ROUGH _____ SMOOTH _____ WOOLLY _____ FLUFFY _____

FURRY _____ BRISTLY _____ SILKY _____ SLIMEY _____

GREASY _____ GRAINY _____ SOFT _____ HARD _____

Activity In the grid below, sketch a representation for each of the textures.

Pattern

Pattern is the element of art that refers to the **repetition** of anything: shape, line, colour, etc. If a certain item is repeated, it can also be referred to as a **motif**.

Patterns can be **man-made** or **organic**. Man-made patterns are geometric and tend to be quite linear and structured; organic patterns show definite repetition, but they are not as uniform and defined.

Activity Draw the following man-made patterns.

| BRICKS | TILES | PIANO KEYS |

Activity Draw the following organic patterns.

| ZEBRA | LEAF | LEOPARD |

Pattern can be used to disguise, e.g. camouflage.

Activity — Draw an example of pattern being used as camouflage.

Motifs can be simple symbols that represent a bigger meaning, e.g. a shamrock is a motif that represents Ireland; a heart is a motif that represents love.

Activity — Draw some motifs and list their meanings.

_____ = _____

_____ = _____

_____ = _____

_____ = _____

William Morris was a nineteenth-century British designer who used a lot of pattern in his work. Many of his prints feature floral designs. A **print** is an easy way to create a pattern because you only have to create one original and then you recreate as many prints as you like from that.

Activity Create a pattern below. You can use a print made from a potato or a piece of lino; you can use your fingerprint; or you can draw a repeated pattern, perhaps using one of the motifs you listed on p.42.

A **monoprint** is a print that leaves only one impression, unlike prints that allow multiples of the same piece to be created (e.g. pieces of potato or lino).

Balance

Balance is a principle of design that describes how artists create visual weight. Artists use art elements such as line, shape and colour to **balance** their work. Balance refers to the way the elements of art are arranged in order to create a feeling of stability in an artwork.

Balance can be:

- **symmetrical** (formal), meaning both sides of an imaginary line are the same.
- **asymmetrical** (informal), meaning both sides of an imaginary line are different but equal in weight.
- **radial**, when lines or shapes grow evenly from a centre point.

Symmetrical Balance

Butterflies are symmetrical because their colour and pattern are the exact same on both sides.

Activity Add colour and pattern to the butterfly.

Asymmetrical Balance

This image of a weighing scale is an example of asymmetrical balance.

Activity Draw an image with asymmetrical balance.

Radial Balance

Mandala is a Sanskrit word meaning 'circle'. *Mandalas* are concentric diagrams that have spiritual and ritual significance in Buddhism and Hinduism. They are used to focus the mind during meditation.

Activity Develop the pattern of this *mandala* and colour it, keeping the balance even.

Space

Two-dimensional space is found on flat surfaces such as paper or canvas. It has no depth, only length and width. However, the same surface can be used to make a two-dimensional object appear three-dimensional by giving the illusion of depth.

When we see a drawing or painting that has the illusion of three-dimensional spaces and forms, it indicates that the artist has used the elements of art and the principles of design in the following ways:

- overlapping objects
- changing size and placement of objects
- perspective
- tone

Perspective

Perspective is used to create an illusion of depth or distance in a picture. **Overlap perspective** refers to objects appearing in front of one another: naturally, the objects become smaller in appearance the further away they are.

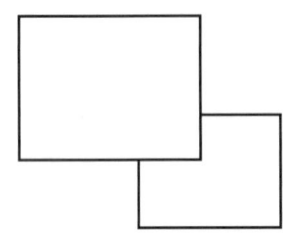

Linear perspective is dependent on a **vanishing point**: the place on the horizon where lines that are parallel in reality meet in order to create the illusion of distance. **One-point perspective** means that there is only one point on the horizon where objects become so small that they disappear. However, an artist may use two or even three points to describe distance in their work. The more vanishing points there are, the more complex the work.

One-point perspective

One-point perspective is evident in the sketch below.

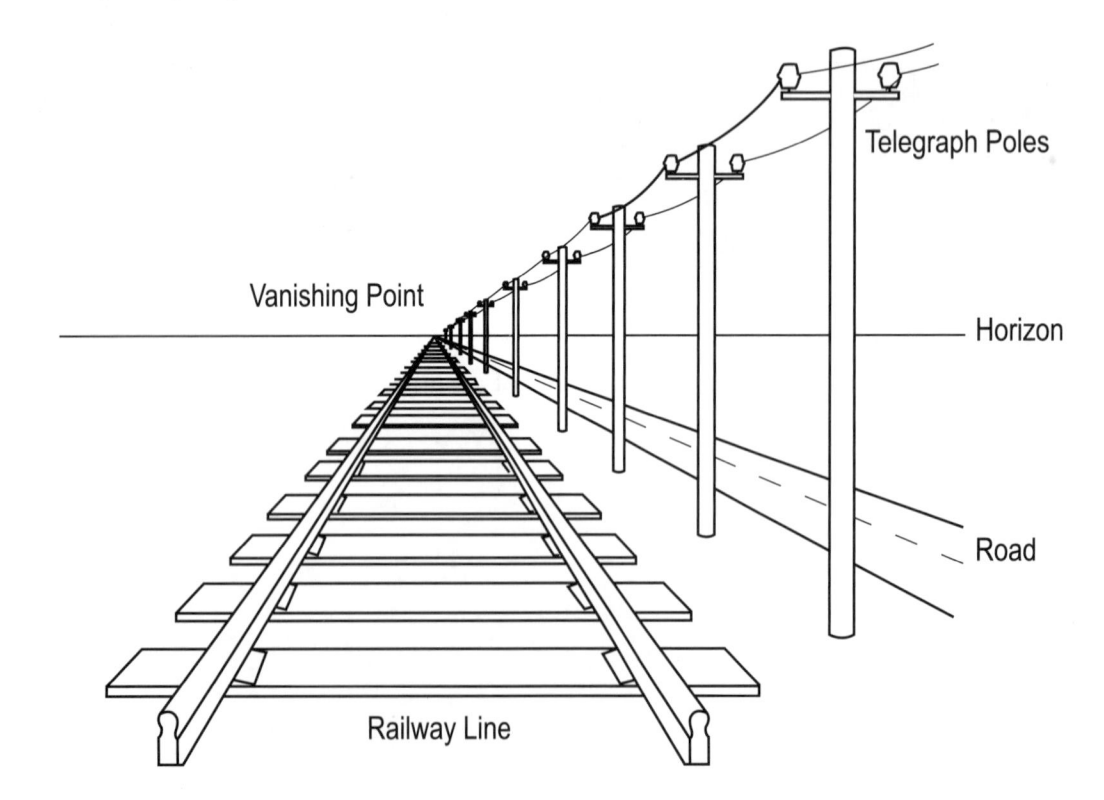

Vanishing Point

Telegraph Poles

Horizon

Road

Railway Line

Two-point perspective

Two-point perspective is evident in the sketch below.

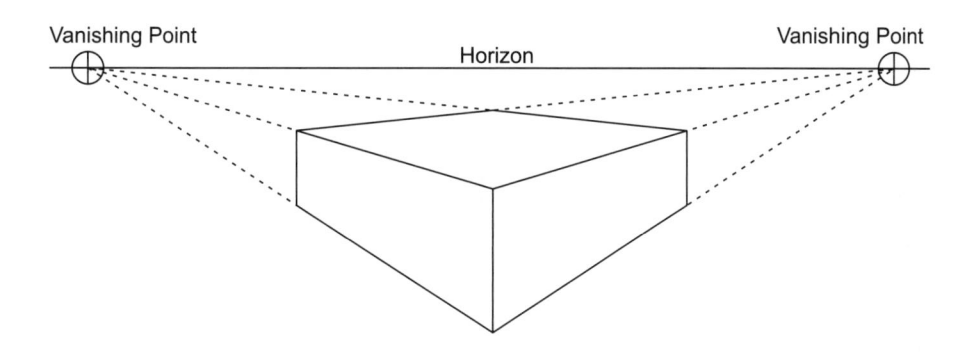

Activity Create a 3D version of your name, using one-point perspective. An example is given here.

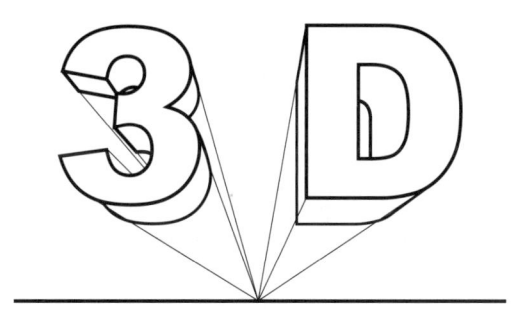

Examine the following sketches to understand the difference between one-point perspective and two-point perspective.

One-point perspective: room.

Activity Recreate the drawing step by step in the large box provided.

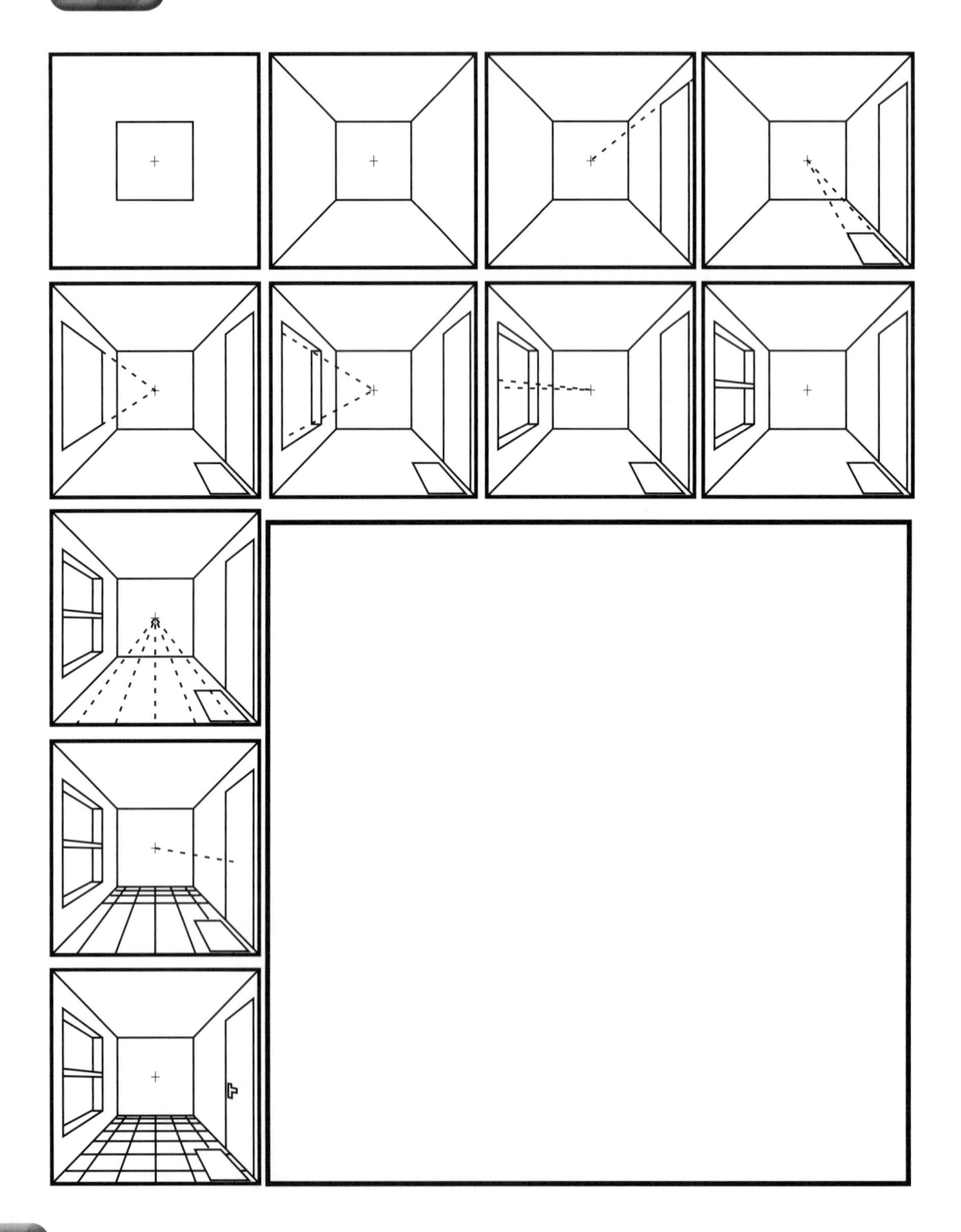

Two-point perspective: building.

Activity Recreate the drawing step by step in the large box below.

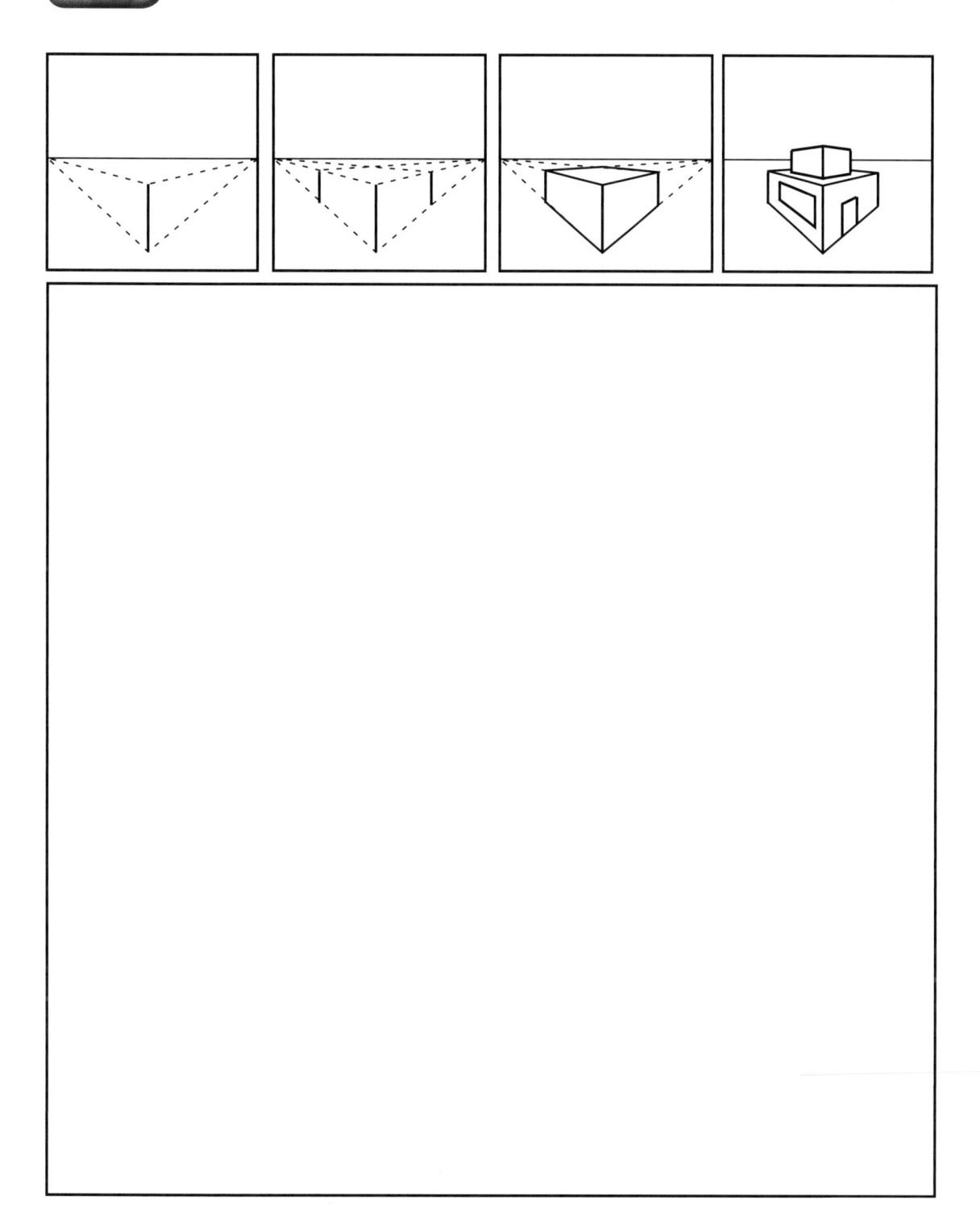

Junior Certificate Art & Design Workbook

Activity Create a drawing that uses *overlapping objects* to give the illusion of three-dimensional space.

Activity Create a drawing that changes *the size and placement of objects* to give the illusion of three-dimensional space.

Activity Create a drawing that uses *perspective* to give the illusion of three-dimensional space.

Activity Create a drawing that uses *tone* to give the illusion of three-dimensional space.

Rhythm

Rhythm is a principle of design that refers to a visual tempo or beat. Like pattern, it is created when there is a regular repetition of art elements (e.g. colour or line). Rhythm produces the feeling of movement. It is often achieved by making the viewer's eye move from one area to the next.

Activity Create a composition that displays the use of rhythm.

Scale

Scale is a principle of design used to express **size relationships** in an artwork. It refers to the proportion or ratio of the elements of the piece. It is particularly useful for architectural plans and maps, which create the illusion of the correct size on a smaller scale.

Activity Draw an image in the small grid and then copy it (box for box) into the larger grid. You will have the exact same image at two different scales. The ratio of these drawings is 1:2.

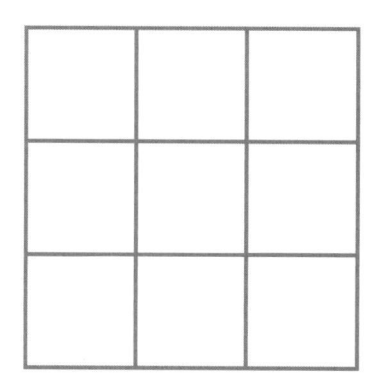

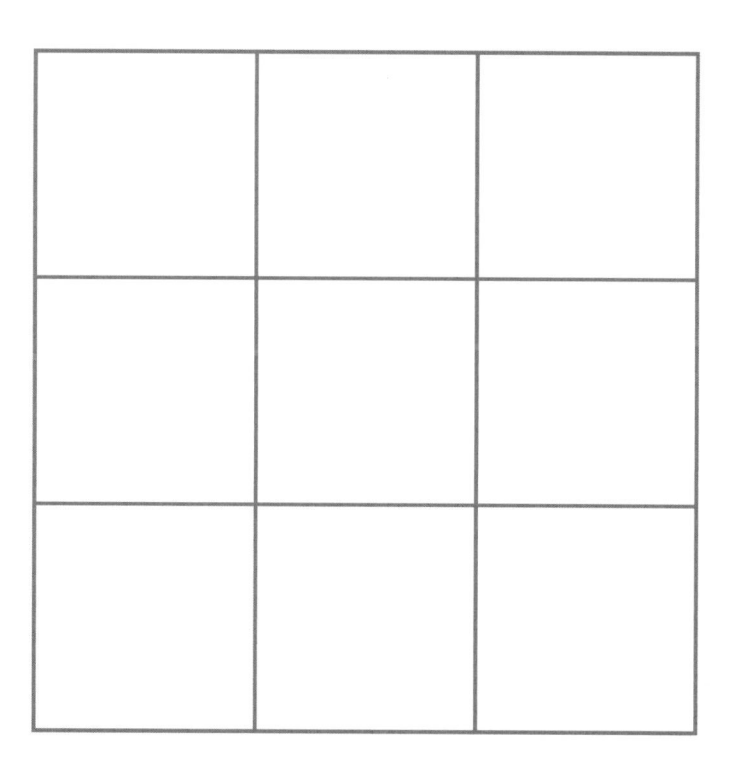

Size

Size is simply the relationship between the area occupied by one shape and the area occupied by another. In order to have large-sized shapes, smaller ones must also be present.

Size differences can create an interesting dynamic within a design. The eye is drawn to larger shapes. Contrasting sizes can create **tension**, which really adds impact to a design.

Activity Create compositions of shapes in the boxes below. Experiment with different sizes and see if you can create tension or harmony.

Emphasis

Emphasis is used to attract attention to certain elements in an artwork. A **focal point** draws the viewer's attention to the most important element in the piece. There are several techniques used to emphasise the most important object in a piece.

Emphasis by contrast: This can be achieved in an artwork that uses all organic shapes, except for a single geometric shape. Sometimes, the use of a particularly strong colour can create a focal point. If an artwork is mostly dark, a splash of light creates a focal point, e.g. the lantern in Caravaggio's *The Taking of Christ*.

Emphasis by isolation: If most of the objects in an artwork are grouped together, another object that stands alone will create a focal point.

Emphasis by placement: An object placed in the centre of an artwork can be a focal point. If an object is placed at the centre of the lines of perspective, the object will appear to be the focus of the work.

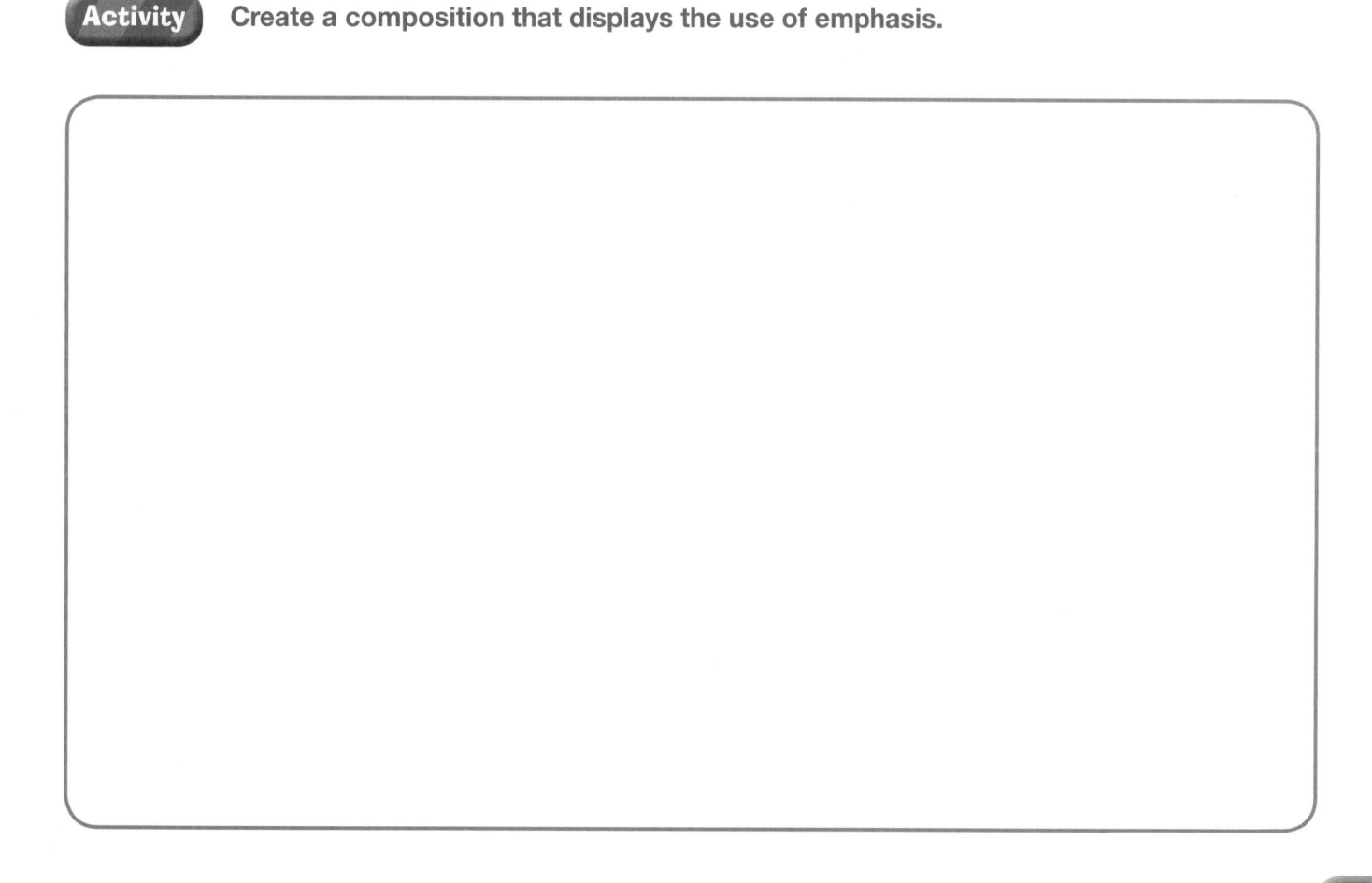

Activity Create a composition that displays the use of emphasis.

Unity

Unity is a measure of how the elements of an artwork seem to **fit together**. Unity can be achieved by use of **proximity**: placing those objects together that appear to belong in a group. **Repetition** can be used to create unity and to tie together the various elements of a piece. **Continuation** is a subtle way of unifying a work: it involves the continuation of line, colour or shape from one area to another.

Activity Create a composition that displays the use of unity.

Composition

Composition is the method by which elements or parts are arranged into an organised and pleasing overall structure. Format plays a part in composition. This book, for instance, is in **portrait** format; turned onto its side, it becomes **landscape** format.

Pictorial composition needs consideration. You can do different things with **focal points**, depending on the effect you want to achieve. You can indicate tension for the viewer by creating a lopsided composition.

It is good to experiment with various compositions before committing to your finished piece. **Thumbnail sketches** are very useful (see p.60). They allow you to make several different small-scale sketches for a piece before you decide on the final layout or composition.

Before you make a decision on composition, it can be useful to examine the **shapes** in your intended piece. Simplify any complex shapes and lay them out in order to create a pattern and rhythm that you consider to be well balanced.

The use of **colour** is very important in your composition, also. Colour can help to create effects of balance and rhythm.

The Rule of Thirds

One way of creating a simple composition is to follow the **rule of thirds**. This involves creating a grid and placing objects of importance on any one of the **four focal points** that are present. Focal points naturally draw the eye of the viewer; and any object placed on any one of the focal points will appear more prominent. The rule of thirds also helps us to identify the **foreground**, **middle ground** and **background**.

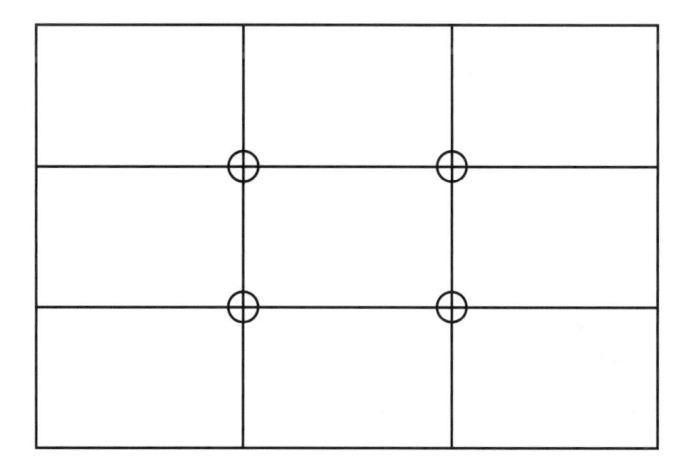

Thumbnail Sketches

Thumbnail sketches will save you time in your design work and they are useful in giving you the opportunity to experiment on a small scale before committing to the large-scale finished piece.

Viewfinder

A viewfinder can help you to decide on the right composition for your piece.
If you don't want to draw a full view, experiment with a viewfinder until you see the composition you want to create. If you don't have a viewfinder, use your hands to find the area you wish to draw!

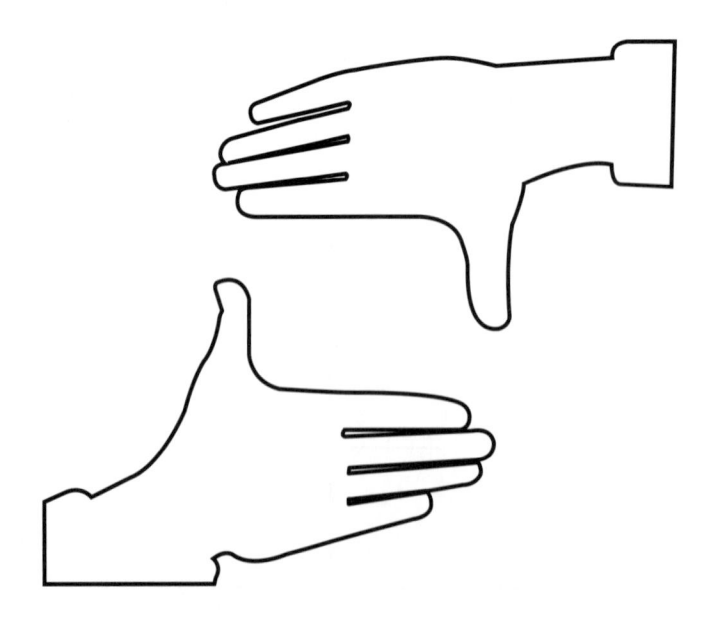

The Telling Triangle

The **telling triangle** is a very basic form of composition. If you are taking a photograph of three people, the most pleasing pose occurs when the tallest person is in the centre. This gives the composition a balanced layout.

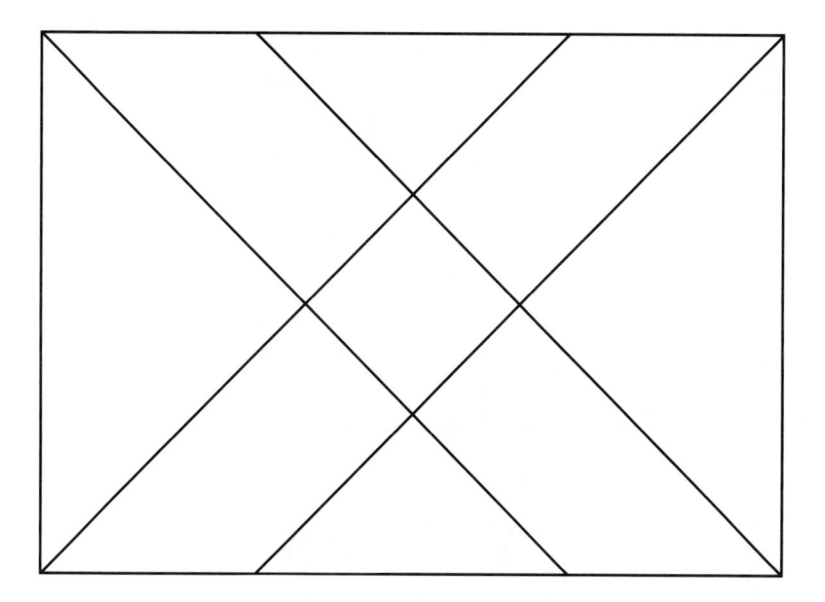

Activity Create a symmetrical composition, using the *telling triangle*.

The Golden Mean

This form of composition creates flow and movement in the work. It directs the eye around the space in a balanced manner because it comes back on itself in an almost circular flow.

Proportion

Proportion refers to the **relative size and scale** of the different parts of an artwork. It has a great deal to do with the overall harmony of a piece of art. Leonardo da Vinci's 'Vitruvian Man' is an example of how artists have tried to create laws of proportion.

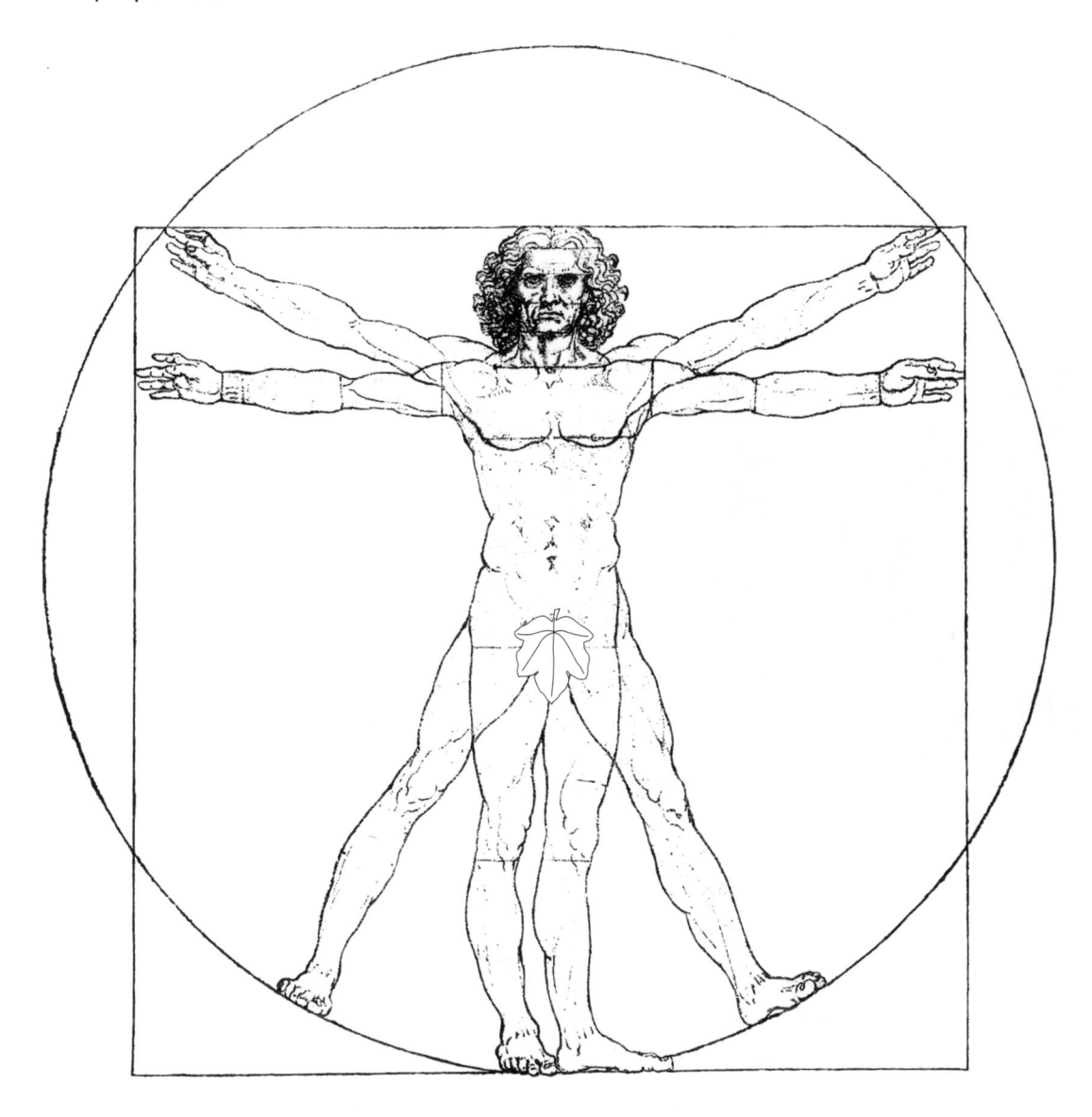

Not only was Leonardo da Vinci a master painter, but he was also an architect and engineer. He had a great interest in science and nature. He also invented many things; he is credited with some of the first drawings of a helicopter.

Activity Do some research to find out more about **Leonardo da Vinci**.

Proportion of the Face

The human face has a set layout. Even though facial features differ from person to person, the positioning of the nose, mouth, eyes and ears (and their size in relation to each other) is the same on every face.

Artists often look at the underlying structure of an object in order to improve their understanding of it before they begin to draw. The same is true for the anatomy of the body and the human skull.

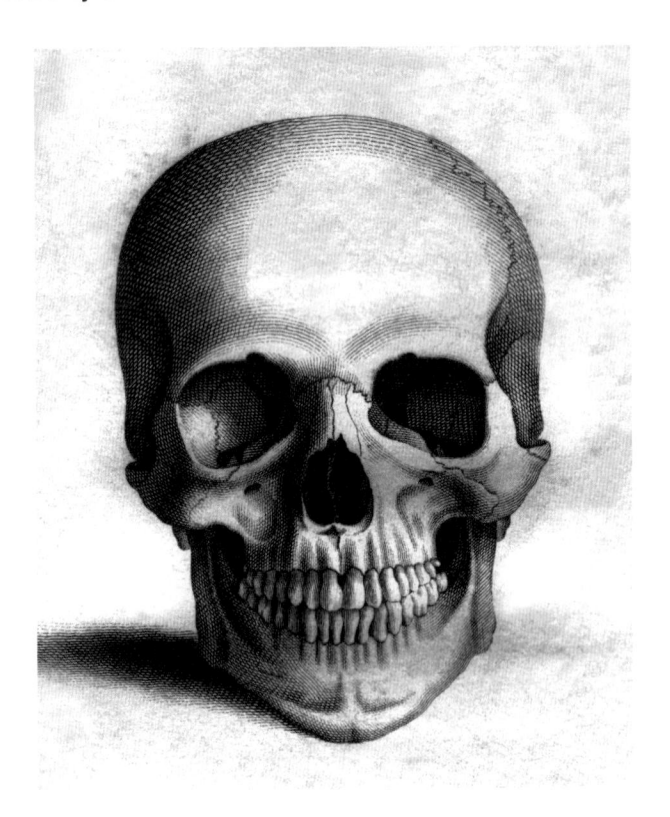

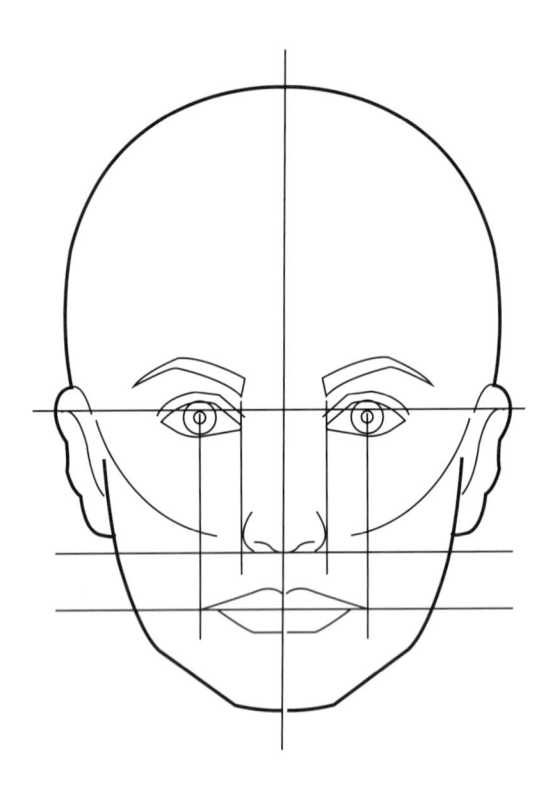

Notice the structure of the human face:

- The **eyes** appear halfway down the head. They are equal in size and symmetrical. The width of the face is the same measurement as five eyes in a row.
- The **nose** appears halfway between the eyes and the chin.
- The **mouth** appears halfway between the nose and the chin.
- The **ears** are the same length as the nose.

Drawing a self-portrait is a great way to practise proportion of the face. All you need is a mirror, pencil and paper – and plenty of time to examine all the features of your face.

Junior Certificate Art & Design Workbook

Activity Choose one of the following facial expressions and base a self-portrait on it.

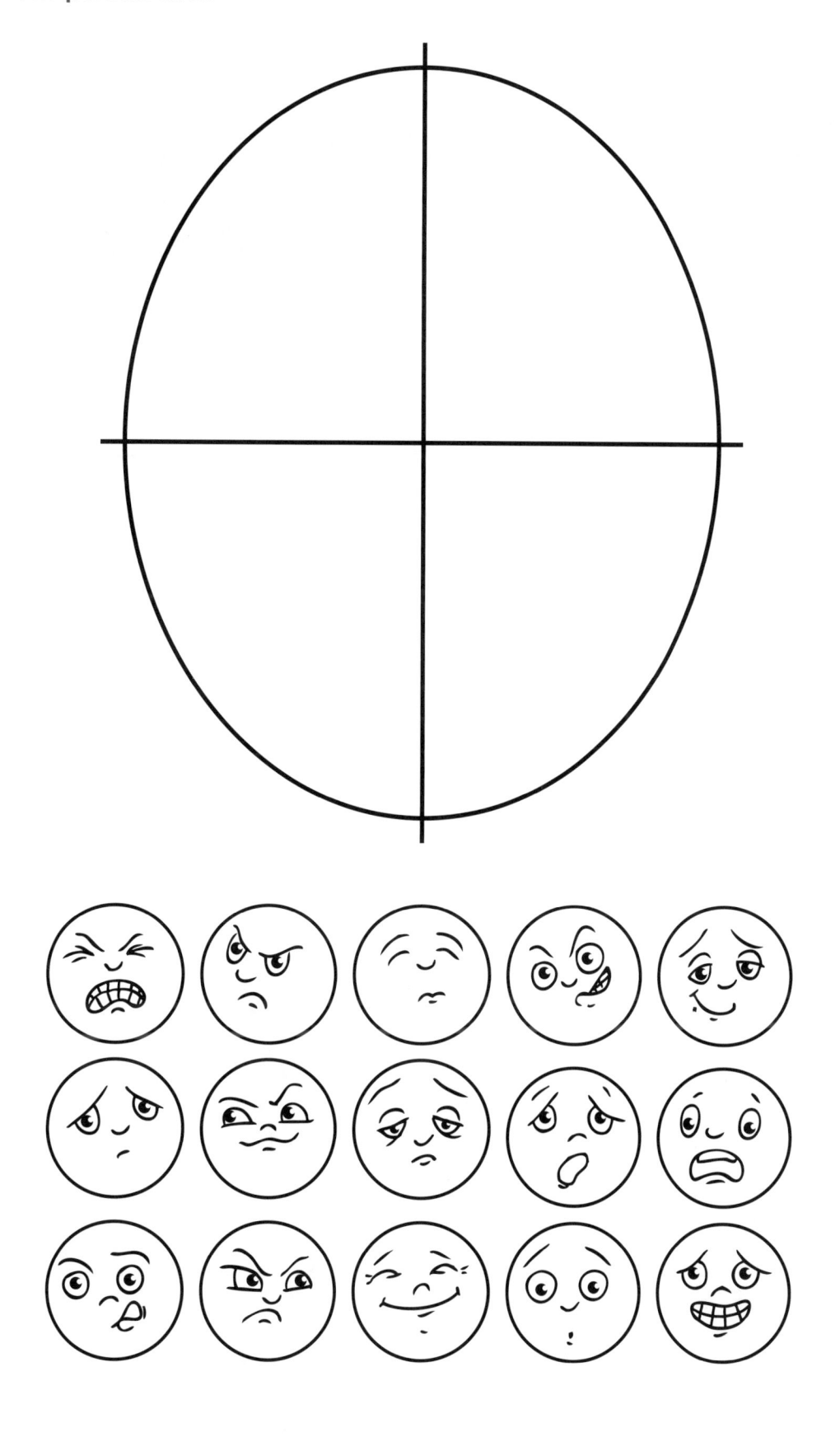

65

Junior Certificate Art & Design Workbook

Activity Draw a face on this WANTED poster. Give it any expression you like and try to use your understanding of proportion.

WANTED

Proportion of the Body

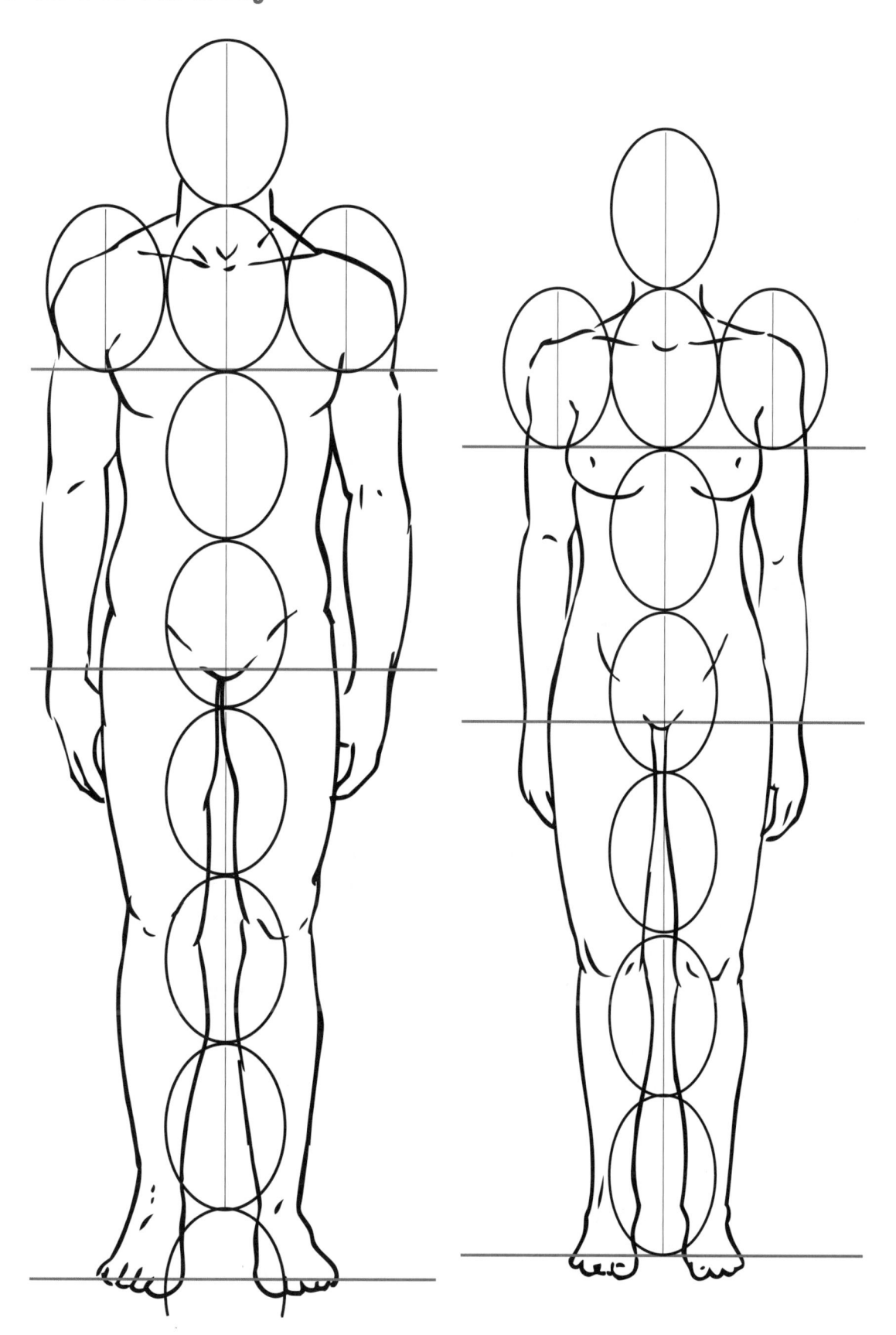

The human body also has set proportions, as shown in the diagram on p.67. Height is usually the length of seven heads in a column. The width of the shoulders is usually the width of three heads in a row. Remembering these rules of proportion will make it much quicker and easier for you to draw people.

Artists often use their *pencils* to help them measure the features of an object or figure and to understand proportions. The way to do this is to choose one area to measure, e.g. the head from the crown to the chin. Hold your pencil in your fist with your arm fully extended (the arm must be straight or you will get a different measurement each time). Hold the pencil in view of the head and mark its height on the pencil with your thumb, then measure how many times that fits into the whole height of the body.

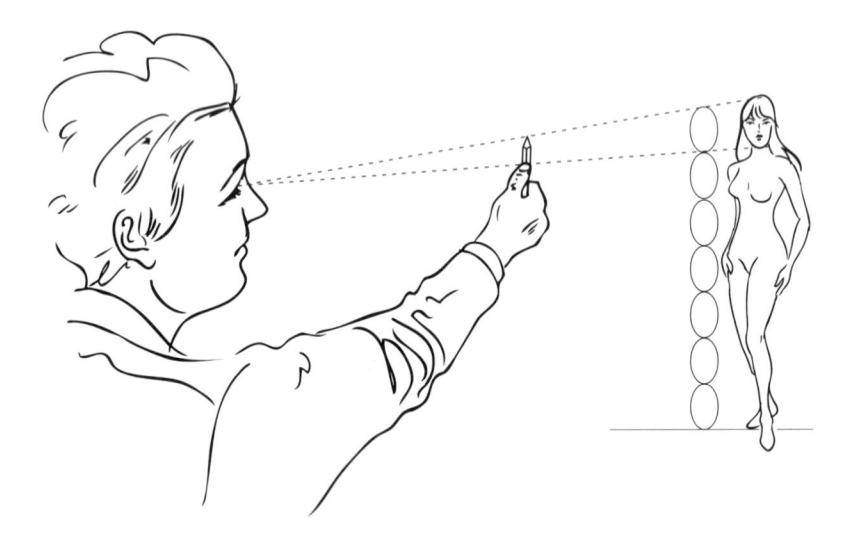

Once you understand the general proportions of the human body and face, you can experiment with different angles and different centres of gravity: action poses or movements that show the body standing off-centre. You can also experiment with **foreshortening**. This is when a feature or limb seems nearer in the picture because of the angle at which it has been drawn; it appears distorted but more correct.

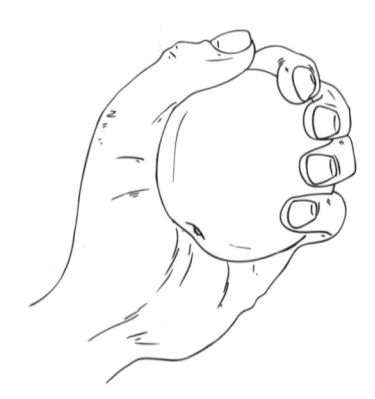

Activity   Draw a full human figure in proportion. Give the body a costume.

The Junior Certificate Art Exam

The Junior Certificate Art exam paper is released for third-year students in October of each year, giving candidates over seven months to put together their finished project. The project is then submitted along with two drawing exams (life drawing and still life) at the beginning of the following May. The same paper is given to Ordinary and Higher Level students, but it is marked differently depending on the level of exam taken. Candidates select one theme from a list of six.

The Project

Project work is made up of **three** components:

- **2D (painting or graphic design)**, e.g. poster; book jacket; video, DVD or CD cover; logo; brochure; postage stamp; etc.
- **3D**, e.g. modelling; carving; or construction.
- **Option (2D or 3D)**, e.g. batik; block printmaking; etching; book craft; calligraphy; embroidery; fabric printing; screen printing; weaving; art metalwork; carving; modelling; casting; packaging; pottery; ceramics; puppetry; etc.

The entire Junior Certificate Art course can be broken into ten sections:

1. Preparation for 2D (painting *or* graphic design)
2. Completed 2D (painting *or* graphic design)
3. Support studies for 2D (painting *or* graphic design)
4. Preparation for 3D
5. Completed 3D
6. Preparation for Option
7. Completed Option
8. Support studies for 3D *and* Option
9. Life drawing (drawing from human form)
10. Still life (drawing from natural/man-made form)

There are **300 marks** assigned to project work.

- **75 marks** for **preparation**: research and investigation using a variety of media.
- **75 marks** for **development**: studies showing individual creative ideas.

- **120 marks** for **realisation**: completed 2D and 3D pieces.
- **30 marks** for **support studies**: visual and written support work relating to the project.

Support Studies

Support studies are things that relate to your project and support your work.

They could refer to the work of **another artist** who has influenced you. They could be **found objects**, e.g. postcards, magazines, packaging, wrapping paper, books, leaflets, calendars, photos, films, newspapers, fashion, architecture or pop culture.

They could be examples of different **techniques** that you would consider using in your work:

- frottage: rubbing over a textured surface, e.g. a coin or gravestone
- collage: 2D composition that uses found materials to create an image
- assemblage: 3D collage
- montage: collage using photographs
- mixed media: using a variety of media, e.g. paint, pencils and markers

It is good practice to create A2-size sheets of support studies and sketches for *all* your projects. Presentation of your work for support studies is just as important as presentation of your finished pieces. Organising the work in a pleasing layout and mounting it on presentation card or paper is very important. Framing each individual sketch (giving it a border) will add to the quality of the presentation.

You will investigate many artists and art movements in your studies and this will influence and support your own work. When studying the work of any artist, ensure that you can elaborate on each of the following:

- names and dates in relation to the artist and art movement
- description of artwork and materials used
- significance of the art movement and the artist's work (socially, politically and historically)
- description of the artist's personal relationships and lifestyle
- your opinion of the artist/artwork and the reasoning behind this
- comparison/contrast of one work with another

Graphic Design

Graphic design is the visual interpretation of an idea or concept.

Drawing is an important design tool, used throughout the entire process and often for the finished product. The broader your understanding of materials and techniques, the better equipped you will be to carry out your idea. This is where **experimentation** with the use of thumbnail sketches is very important. Thumbnail sketches help you to come up with multiple solutions to any design problem; and they enable you to plan, organise and analyse the design properly.

With graphic design, you can apply all the elements of art and the principles of design. Document all your ideas in your journal or sketch pad and continue to document developments as the design progresses.

Visual Communication

Symbols can communicate ideas in a visual way.

Activity Examine the following symbols and think about the meaning of each one. Can you add suitable colour to any of the symbols? What does the colouring symbolise?

Lettering

One of the most important areas of graphic design is **lettering**. Learning how to create and use different styles of lettering is vital for graphic design.

This diagram shows the development of the alphabet from pictures to the letters we recognise today.

CRETAN PICTO-GRAPHS	PHOE-NICIAN	EARLY GREEK	CLASSICAL GREEK	LATIN	MODERN ENGLISH
∀	⩜	A	A	A	**A**
⌂	9	ꓭ	B	B	**B**
⌒	1	1	Γ	C	**C**
△	⊲	△	△	D	**D**
目	⇉	⇉	E	E	**E**

You can be very creative with the use of lettering. Fonts (typefaces) come in hundreds of varieties on computer programs, providing endless opportunity for experimentation.

Fonts Fonts *Fonts*
FONTS **Fonts**
Fonts Fonts **Fonts**
Fonts **Fonts** Fonts
FONTS Fonts
Fonts *Fonts*
Fonts **Fonts**
FONTS FONTS
Fonts *fonts* Fonts

Activity Choose a font from any book – even this one! Draw the letters A to Z in the grid below and experiment with different colours. Some letters are similar and can be grouped together to make drawing easier: O, C, G, D, Q, S; and H, L, T, F, E. Can any other letters be grouped together?

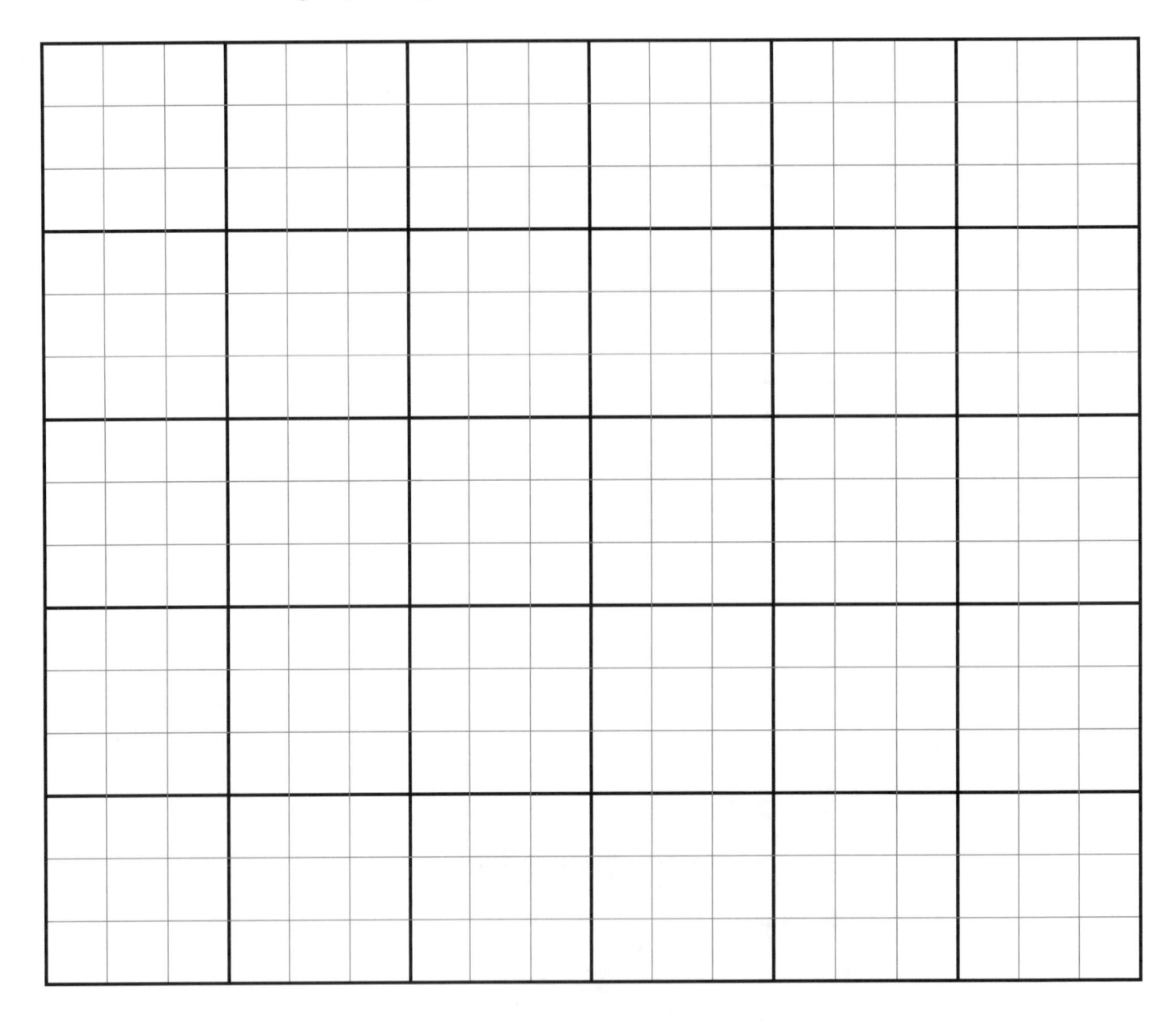

Typography is the art of creating typefaces (fonts). You can take a basic set of lettering and render it by adding or subtracting detail to create something original. Expressive typography creates the letter as an image. You will notice expressive typography in packaging design.

Activity Represent the following words with expressive lettering:
FAST, ROUGH, SHARP, ICE, SPIRAL, ORANGE, TRIANGLE, SUN, FLUFFY.

Try adding colour to convey your ideas more effectively.

Junior Certificate Art & Design Workbook

The **placement of words** within a piece of graphic design can also be expressive. Consider the following:

- overlapping
- cropping
- positive and negative shape
- elaboration
- repetition
- intersecting
- relationship to frame
- touching
- size

Hanging

broken

echo echo echo

Activity Draw the following words in expressive typography:
LINE, SMALL, STEEP, POP, FULL, HALF, HIDDEN, DIVIDE, REVERSE.

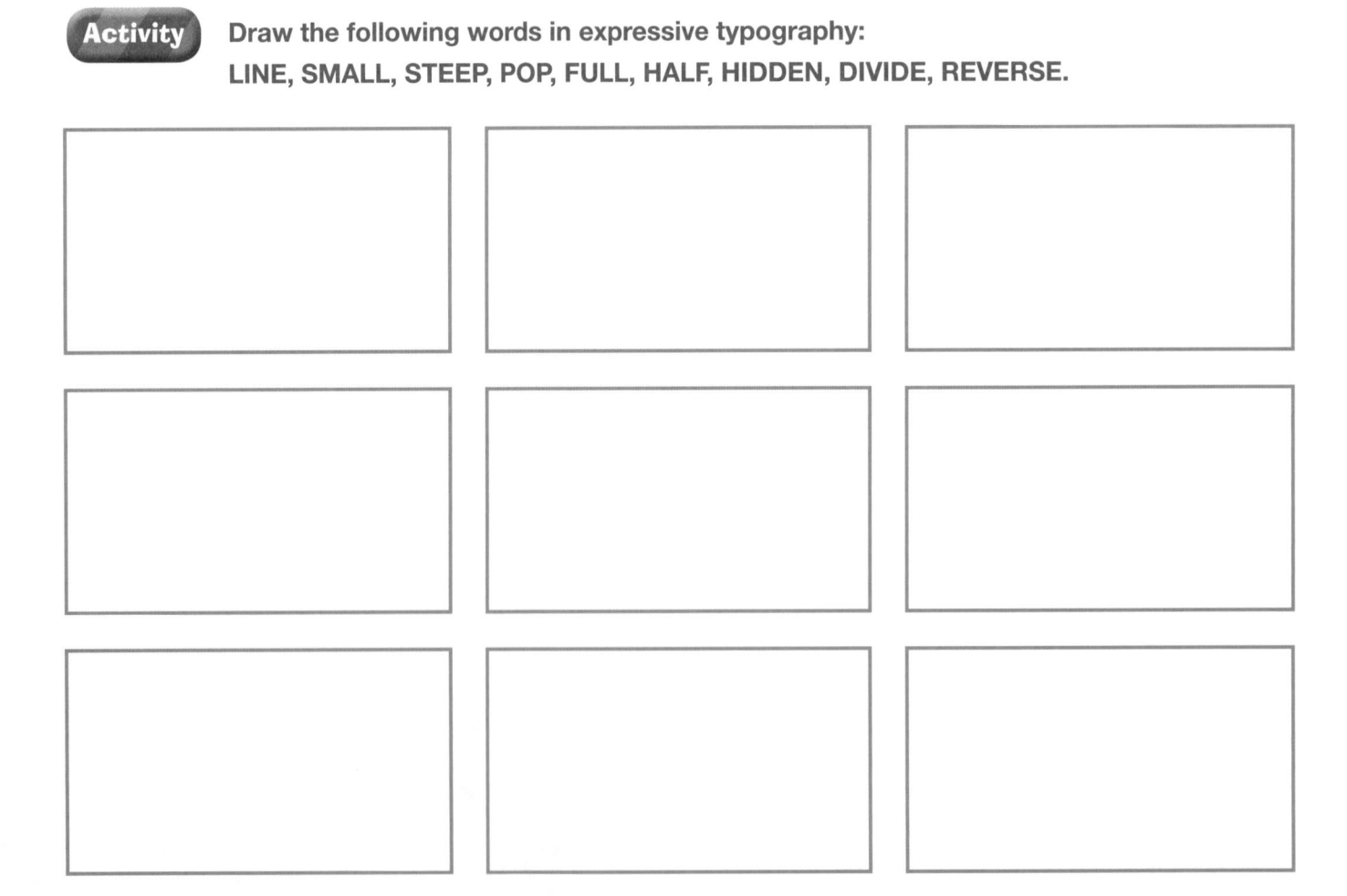

Calligraphy

Calligraphy

Calligraphy is an ancient art form and the word simply means 'beautiful lettering'. There are many different varieties and styles. Calligraphy pens have a flat edge, in contrast to the point of a regular pen. A calligraphy pen must be held at a 45-degree angle.

Calligraphy Fonts a b c d e f

Brush Script A B C d e f g

Apple Chancery 1 2 3

Lucidia Aa Bb Cc

Edwardian Dd Ee Ff Gg

𝔅𝔩𝔞𝔠𝔨𝔩𝔢𝔱𝔱𝔢𝔯 𝔄 𝔅 ℭ 𝔡

Zapfino a b c d e f g h i j

Activity Create some calligraphy. If you do not have a calligraphy pen, experiment with taping two pencils together or use a flat piece of wood or bamboo.

You could do a finished piece based on a poem you are studying for English class.

Logo

A logo is a symbol that represents a group or an individual; it is like a motif. Your family may have a coat of arms or a crest, which is a logo of sorts for the family name.

Activity Draw your family crest below; or design a new one with symbols that represent your family.

Business logos often incorporate an image that represents the product or service supplied by the company. Can you think of any logos for cars, fast food restaurants, sports teams or clothes?

Activity Imagine you are starting a business. Create a business logo that would represent your company.

Packaging

Packaging is a form of advertising. Styles of packaging vary for many reasons: brand image, budget, functionality, durability and ease of use. Many clever and practical examples of packaging can be seen on the internet and in shops. Expressive typography and interesting design forms are a part of packaging. You can download templates of packaging boxes online.

If you are designing your own packaging, you need to think about the:

- product you intend to market
- target age group (choose age-appropriate colours and text)
- budget available
- materials that are most suitable

Activity List different products and the packaging that is most suitable for them.

Product

_____

_____

_____

_____

Packaging

_____

_____

_____

_____

Junior Certificate Art & Design Workbook

Activity Design packaging for a box of sweets.

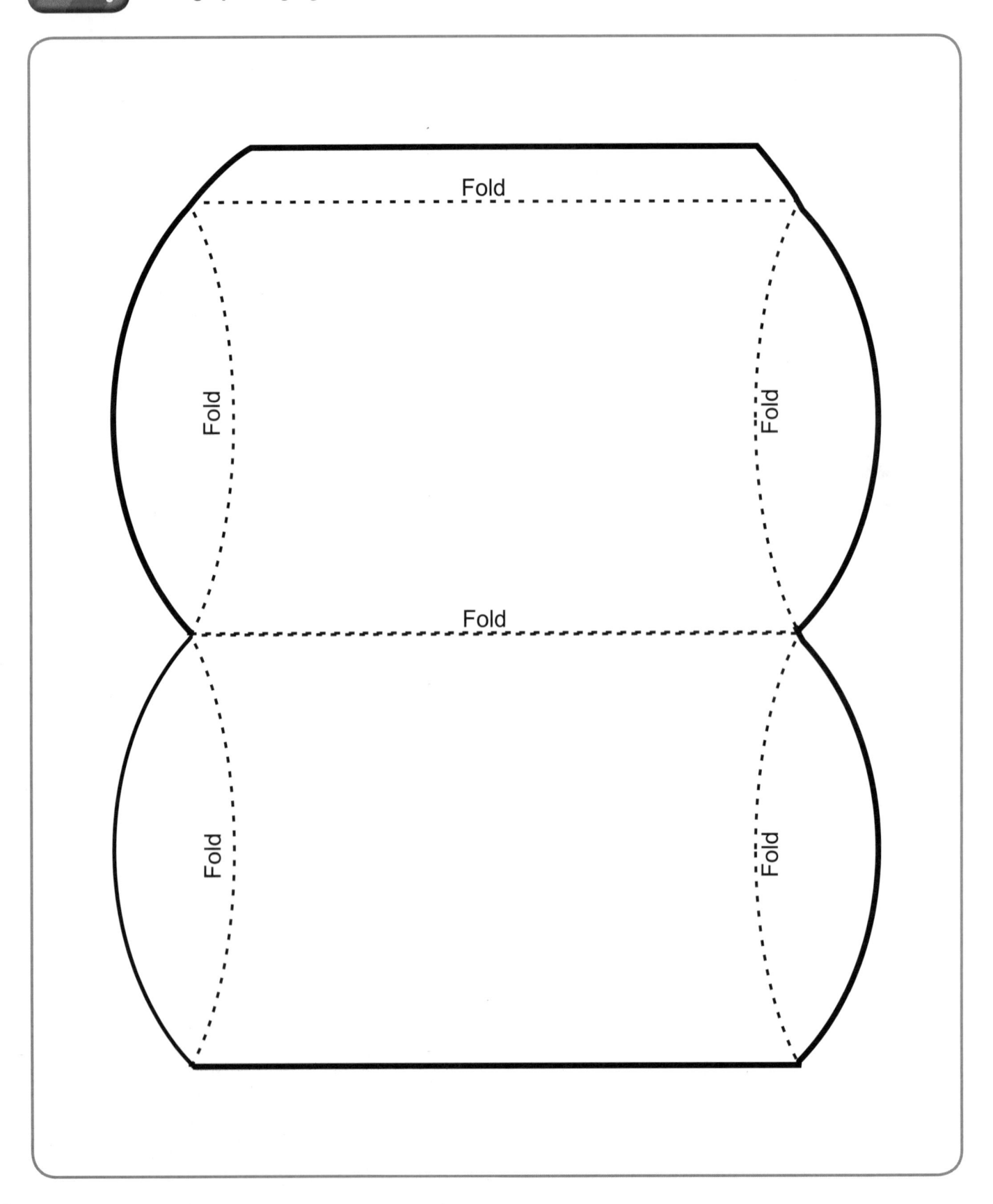

Fold

Fold

Fold

Fold

Fold

Fold

Poster

The aim of a poster is to attract viewers and impart a message. It is important to get the balance right between the text and image. Limit the amount of information to what is essential.

Posters are a means of **visual communication**, used to convey information to a target audience. If they are done well, they are a quick and effective way to communicate a message. They can display clever use of slogans/catchphrases, the elements of art and the principles of design.

Advertising and marketing companies spend a lot of money on poster campaigns. Designs can be made to be site-specific, e.g. a poster on the bus could be designed specifically to appeal to commuters using that service.

Centring Text

Many posters have the text centred. This can be done easily with computer programs but it is useful to know how to do this by hand.

First, divide the page down the centre and rule a line across the page where you intend your text to sit.

Next, count the number of characters, e.g. letters, spaces and numbers. For example, BAKE SALE has 9 characters, including the space between the two words. The centre line for this will be the space between the E of BAKE and S of SALE. There are four characters on either side of the centre line, so we mark four equal-sized spaces on each side.

Now, working from the centre line outwards, add the text. From centre to left, we place the letters E, K, A, B and from centre to right we place the characters S, A, L, E.

Activity Centre the text BAKE SALE in the box below.

Junior Certificate Art & Design Workbook

Activity

Create a poster for your favourite band. Include the name of the band and details of their next concert: date, venue and price of tickets. Include an image. (It doesn't have to be a picture of the band; a related image will do.)

First, do thumbnails sketches to experiment with various layouts; then draw your finished image in the large box.

Postage Stamps

Before the invention of stamps, people *receiving* a letter would pay for the service on receipt. The first pre-paid postage stamps were invented in England in 1840. They cost one penny and showed the profile of Queen Victoria. This stamp became known as the 'Penny Black' because of its colour and price. It is the rarest stamp in the world today and is a collector's item.

Commemorative stamps are stamps designed to pay tribute to a special occasion, person or historical event. Some people keep stamp collections. Stamps from different countries can vary greatly in terms of shape, size and the images used. Rare stamps can be very valuable.

Activity Find some used stamps with interesting designs and glue them below.

Junior Certificate Art & Design Workbook

Activity Design a commemorative stamp for an occasion of your choice. Include text to show the country of origin and the price.

First, do thumbnails sketches to experiment with various layouts; then draw your finished design in the large box.

87

Printmaking

Printmaking began with Johannes Gutenberg's invention of the moveable type printing press around 1439. Nowadays, we take for granted that we have newspapers, magazines and books; but there was a time when many people couldn't read and the only materials available to read were handwritten manuscripts, e.g. The Book of Kells.

A **print** is something that we make by impressing an object onto something wet like paint or ink, and then printing it onto another surface, e.g. footprints, fingerprints or shoeprints.

There are various ways of making prints:

- lino print
- engraving
- vegetable print
- etching
- monoprint

Activity Use one of the techniques listed above to create a print.

Textiles

Batik is a traditional way of dyeing fabric. It involves using a wax-resist dyeing technique in order to create a pattern. This method is often used in Indonesian and African textiles.

Embroidery is the art of decorating fabric or material with a needle and thread, in order to create pattern, design or writing.

Fabric printing is the process of applying colour to fabric in order to create definite patterns or designs.

Screen printing is a printing technique that involves using a wire mesh to support an ink-blocking stencil. A squeegee is moved across the stencil, forcing the ink to transfer through the mesh and create the print.

Weaving involves the production of fabric: items such as thread are interlaced in order to form material.

Puppetry is a form of theatre or performance that involves using small dolls or puppets.

Book Cover

Here is an example of a layout of a book cover.

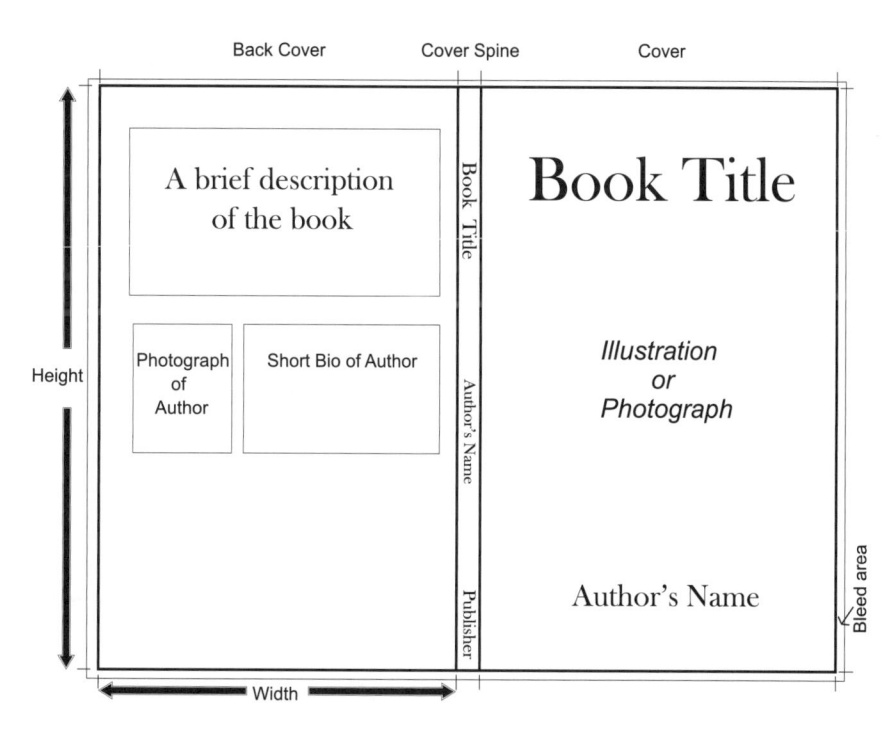

Junior Certificate Art & Design Workbook

Activity Design a book cover in the template below.

3D Studies

You will undertake various 3D projects for the Junior Certificate. It is important to experiment with a variety of materials. Projects could include:

- creating armatures or skeleton frames on which you can build, e.g. modelling wire
- using papier-mâché to reinforce structures
- moulding plaster of Paris or modroc
- creating vessels from clay, using coiling, pinching and slabbing techniques
- using cardboard to create a construction
- making a clay tile in relief with features added on and carved away
- making a base and building a model figure using clay or plasticine
- using found materials to create a model, carving or construction

There are three main processes for 3D artwork.

- **Additive:** entails adding material, e.g. clay onto wire to create a model.
- **Subtractive:** entails removing material, e.g. carving into wood.
- **Constructional:** entails building or putting together materials, e.g. cardboard.

Art and the Community

There are many ways in which the visual arts are alive in our communities. Art groups meet at local libraries and community centres. Town councils put in place sculptures and permanent artworks around the locality. Galleries and exhibition spaces display artworks. Individual members of the community often show great creativity and artistic flair in the ways in which they decorate their homes and gardens.

Activity Make a list of the art resources present in your community.

Activity Organise an art event in your community, e.g. ask a local artist to visit your school; arrange a trip to a local art exhibition; or organise a sale of artworks made by you and your classmates.

Evaluation

As you continue your journey in art and design, you will develop a unique style of your own. It is important to learn how to critique your own work and the work of others in a respectful way that will help you to understand what appeals to you. You need to practise making a personal response to artwork and to speculate about meaning and symbolism in art on a regular basis.

You will learn to interpret works of art by **raising questions**. Remember that no question is too silly or too serious. If you take this approach, you will learn to feel confident in using the vocabulary of visual art.

In your journal or sketch pad, keep written notes of your reactions to works you encounter. Here are some things you should consider when evaluating the success of a project you have completed.

- Did you pick a theme that kept your interest?
- Did you research well?
- Did you manage your time well?
- Did you pick the right materials?
- Which of the elements of art and the principles of design did you use?
- What art skills were used?
- What future projects could relate to this project?
- Did the project relate to your environment: socially, culturally, personally, economically?

Art Timeline

Activity Research the history of art and fill in the names of key artists/key artworks.

ART TIMELINE (approx.)		KEY ARTISTS/KEY ARTWORKS
Prehistoric	(30000–3000 BC)	_____
Egyptian	(3200–1070 BC)	_____
Byzantine	(1000 BC–330 AD)	_____
Romanesque	(500–1200)	_____
Gothic	(1100–1450)	_____
Renaissance	(1400–1600)	_____
Mannerism	(1527–1580)	_____

Baroque (1600–1700)

Rococo (1700–1750)

Neoclassicism (1750–1880)

Romanticism (1800–1880)

Realism (1830–1870)

Impressionism (1870–1890)

Post Impressionism (1880–1920)

Modernism (1880–1945)

Expressionism (1890–1920)

Les Nabis (1890–1900)

Art Nouveau (1890–1905)

Fauvism (1903–1907)

Cubism (1907–1914)

Dadaism (1916–1922)

Bauhaus (1920–1940)

Surrealism (1924–1930)

Abstract Expressionism (1945–1960)

Pop Art (1960s)